3 — 16 — 66

ECONOMIC LIBERALISM

THE CLASSICAL VIEW

STUDIES IN ECONOMICS

CONSULTING EDITOR: *William Letwin*

MASSACHUSETTS INSTITUTE OF TECHNOLOGY

ECONOMIC
LIBERALISM

Volume II

THE CLASSICAL VIEW

WILLIAM D. GRAMPP
UNIVERSITY OF ILLINOIS, CHICAGO

RANDOM HOUSE   NEW YORK

TO THE MEMORY OF

J. F. G.

FOREWORD

This book consists of six studies in the history of the idea of economic liberalism—three in the first volume and three in the second volume. That may seem like six studies in ambiguity. "Liberalism" has so many meanings—is such a rich source of controversy and inconclusion—that it has become nearly an un-word or an antiword, one that means nothing or even less. Nevertheless, I want to use it. Although it has been used ambiguously, the idea for which it can be made to stand is not ambiguous. It is a word like those words of ordinary language that the linguistic philosophers say we should use, or if it is not like them it can be made so. It has had a meaning in the past, and the history of that meaning can be studied. The economic aspect of the *history* is what this book is about. What economic liberalism means today is not the subject of the book. That is an important question, needless to say, but is one on which the reader will have to do his own thinking. There are some suggestions to help him in the concluding study. As a guide to all of them I would put before him what Berkeley offered to the readers of *The Principles of Human Knowledge:*

Whoever therefore designs to read the following sheets, I entreat him that he would make my words the occasion of his own thinking, and endeavor to attain the same train of thoughts in reading that I had in writing them. By this means it will be easy for him to discover the truth or falsity of what I say. He will be out of all danger of being deceived by my words, and I do not see how he can be led into an error by considering his own naked, undisguised ideas.

I use the words "economic liberalism" to mean the policy that directs a liberal economy, and the words "liberal economy" to mean an economy in which individuals decide what is to be produced, how goods shall be distributed, and by what means production and distribution shall be carried on. Decisions of this kind must be made in some way or other in every kind of economic system, no matter how dictatorial or democratic or how rich or poor. What distinguishes one system from another is whether or not individuals have the ultimate authority to make decisions. *Who* has the authority is more important than *how* it is exercised or for *what* purpose. In a liberal economy, individuals have the authority. They may exercise their authority individually on the market or outside the market, or they may exercise it collectively and voluntarily in either way. They also may exercise their authority through the government by directing it to carry out the decisions they have made. They may go further and delegate to the government the authority to make decisions. What they may not do is to delegate authority in an irrevocable way. They may not turn over to the government, to a voluntary organization, or to another individual the permanent power to make decisions. They must retain the ultimate authority to judge those who act for them.

In a liberal economy the choice of how to make decisions is not necessarily a choice between government and the market and it is not even a choice among different combinations of government and market. Between the two there are many forms of voluntary collective action such as that of cooperatives, philanthropies, nonprofit organizations, limited-profit firms, quasi-public or quasi-private organizations, and unions. In groups of this kind, individuals can change the composition of the national output, the way it is produced, and the way it is distributed.

In the history of economic liberalism, what has been advocated and practiced is a combination of the following three procedures: voluntary individual action on the market, compulsory action through the government, and collective action in voluntary groups. In deciding how these three procedures are to be combined, the critical question usually has been, How much use shall be made of government? The question, in more familiar language, is, What shall be the economic powers of the government?

The question has been answered in different ways by those who have advocated liberalism. But the answers do have a common element. It became apparent in the nineteenth century in Great Britain and it was intimated much earlier. The conclusion to which my studies have brought me is that in a liberal economy the state may do whatever the people want it to do and that it is able to do. Neither the want of the individuals nor the ability of the state is in itself the limit of economic policy. Together they are. The distinction is perhaps obvious. But I have found, during a long period of reading about economic policy, that if the writer had made some obvious distinctions, both he and I would have come to the point with less effort. What a state is *able* to do, as distinct from what it *should* do, is something to be learned from positive economics; it is the analysis of means for achieving given ends. What the state *should* do is a question of ethical values. They once were a part of economics, when economics itself was a branch of moral philosophy. That part is normative economics, and today it still engages the interest of economists even though they attend more to the positive side. Both parts supply the ideas on which economic policy is based. Both have led me to my conclusion about the meaning of economic liberalism—a conclusion that is explained in detail in the chapter "Liberalism in the Great Century."

It is not a conclusion that will be agreeable to everyone. There will be doubts from my colleagues in the history of ideas, and from general readers who have learned elsewhere that liberalism was quite another thing from what it is made out to be here, and from those to whom liberalism is an issue of policy today and of more than historic interest. All of us become committed to ideas, and ideas, it has been truly said, do rule the world. But the commitment can be a vested interest, and ideas can prevent the world and ourselves from learning more. That is why, when we come across an idea that seems eccentric, we ought to try, as Berkeley advised, "to attain the same train of thoughts in reading" as the author had in writing and in this way "to discover the truth or falsity" of what he says.

What I have written in these two volumes is about one aspect of the idea of freedom. A particular definition of freedom is implied by the meaning I have ascribed to economic liberalism. Freedom, in the meaning given it here, is both the absence of restraint upon action and the ability to act. These studies in economic liberalism are therefore studies in the expression of this meaning of freedom. They explain what freedom, in its economic aspect, has meant to particular groups of writers whose ideas have been notably influential. Some of these writers were economists, but most were not. Economics as a distinct study is only about 200 years old, but ideas about the economic aspect of freedom go back much further. Most of the men whose writings are explained here were philosophers, moralists, historians, politicians, experts in statecraft, and pamphleteers. No one of the six studies describes the idea of economic liberalism in its entirety, because no single group of writers made a complete statement about it. What each group had to say is best understood as a statement of particular aspects of the doctrine. To extend these particulars into a synthetic statement of the doctrine is possible but to attribute the synthesis to all of the groups would be quite wrong. One can, however, make a summary statement of the central idea, and I have done that in the last chapter of Volume II. What is just as interesting is to examine the contributions of particular groups of writers at different periods in the development of the idea.

What follows is a brief commentary on each of the six studies in order that the reader may see the design of the whole.

THE STOIC ORIGINS OF LIBERALISM

It was the contribution of the Stoics to explain how individuals must act in order to make their society free. The important feature of Stoicism is the conception of the free individual as a thinking, responsible, and courageous being. But Stoicism was more than a doctrine of individual morality. Political philosophers have long been interested in it, and here I have tried to show the interest it can have for economists.

THE MERCANTILISTS AS LIBERALS

The ideas of political and economic individualism went into decline in the Middle Ages but were not entirely forgotten. They survived in an attenuated form and regained some of their power toward the end of the period. By 1500 they had become a principal doctrine in England. They did not govern the affairs of state, to be sure, but they were ideas that men talked much about and looked forward to putting into practice. The year 1500 was near the start of the period of the mercantilist writers in England, and they have come down to us as the very opposite of liberalism. That view is wrong. There has been a renewed interest in the mercantilists in the last twenty years or so, but mostly by those who believe the mercantilists were superior to the liberals. This view is yet another expression of the mistaken idea that the two had nothing in common.

The mercantilist writers were more familiar with the mechanics of the market and the affairs of state than have been most writers on economic policy. Some of the mercantilists were in business and government, and most of them wrote about specific problems and measures of policy rather than about the principles underlying policy. They were not responsible for the practices of the mercantilist period, many of which were inconsistent with what the writers believed. Their responsibility was for the liberal ideas the period entertained. But the ideas were influenced by what the writers saw around them and by what they experienced directly. There was a close relationship between what the writers saw and their ideas about how to change it—between economic problems and economic policies. This relationship is what makes the writers continually interesting. They were practitioners of economic policy.

THE ORIGINS OF AMERICAN LIBERALISM

Even more significant as practitioners were the Americans of the constitutional period. The influence of British liberalism was greater in the U. S. at this time than in Britain itself. "The colonies owe to the policy of Europe the education and great views of their active and enterprising founders," Smith said. That Smith should have said it is appropriate, because he was the most important single influence on the men who wrote and debated the Constitution and first put it into practice. The fact is interesting because ever since the Constitution was ratified we have been debating the economic intention of the men who wrote it. The intention was, I believe, rather like that of Smith, but his intention was different from what it usually is thought to have been.

THE CLASSICAL PSYCHOLOGY OF LIBERALISM

In the writings of Adam Smith and the classical economists the idea of economic liberalism was expressed most amply and with the greatest power, so much so that the idea often is thought to have come into being in the eighteenth century. It did not, but the statement made of it by the classical economists was the most important. For that reason more of this book is about the eighteenth and nineteenth centuries than any other period. What Smith is best known for, although he probably did not want to be, is the belief that self-interest is the principal motive of economic behavior. I have tried to explain just what he meant by self-interest and have taken special care with the exceptions he took to it.

THE POLITICAL IDEAS OF THE CLASSICAL ECONOMISTS

The economic policy of the classical school was made up of its ideas of psychology, positive economics, of political philosophy and of ethics. The policy was not a simple application of the idea of self-interest, which itself was far from being simple. At first sight there seems to be no consistency among the ideas. Indeed there seems to be a fundamental discrepancy between the classicists' believing in universal economic freedom but not in universal political freedom and in their being advocates of both free trade and political nationalism. But on examination a consistency does emerge. A study of how the classicists related the economic and political aspects of liberalism brings to our notice some features of it that are not apparent from a study of either aspect alone.

LIBERALISM IN THE GREAT CENTURY

The nineteenth century is the notable period in the history of liberalism as a doctrine and practice. That is not to say that liberalism has declined since then. I do not believe it has. But in the nineteenth century its distinctive features became clear and it divided rather sharply into its classic and utilitarian forms. The century was the time of Ricardo and Mill, of the economic supremacy of Great Britain, and the liberal awakening in other countries. It also was the first time that the British government intervened in the economy in a modern way. It usually did so with the approval of the liberal economists. To understand the liberalism of this period we should know something about the particular forms of intervention—the actual practice of policy—in addition to knowing what the ideas of the period were. In other studies I have not described the practice of policy, but in this I have. From a study of the ideas of policy and its practice one can deduce certain principles. I have put the principles together in a summary statement of what liberalism came to mean in the nineteenth century. I take the statement to be its meaning today also. The statement is Part III of the last chapter of the second volume and is entitled "The Meaning of Economic Liberalism."

Each of the six chapters of the book is meant to be a fairly complete statement of the idea of economic liberalism, or of a major aspect of it, as it was expressed at a particular period in its history. But not every period is included here, and so the book is not a complete history of the idea. It omits much. There is nothing, for example, about liberal ideas in the Middle Ages. Other than a few references, there is nothing about economic liberalism on the Continent. There is nothing about the most conspicuous of all versions of liberalism—that associated with the Manchester School of economics. With the exception of the last, about which I have written another book. I have omitted these periods either because they are not so important as those that are included or because I have nothing to say about them which is sufficiently important or interesting to engage the reader's attention.

In writing these studies I have had several purposes. One is to present information to those who, like myself, are interested in the development of economics. Most histories of the subejct say something about policy, especially liberal policy, but not in a way that seems to me to do justice to the ideas. I have wanted also to call attention to the ethical and political elements in economic policy and so to help in some way to create interest in political economy as a subject that is complementary to and not competitive with economic analysis. Analysis has become a formidable discipline and intellectually most respectable, but it still is what it always has been—a means of solving problems and not a field of inquiry that is its own justification. To solve problems we need to know more than positive economics. We also must know something about the political values that set the limits to the solutions. Every economist acknowledges this, even to the point of paying his respects to political economy. But much more effort is put into the positive side of economics than into the normative. It is

effort of a very high order, and one wishes that some of it
would be directed to normative economics.

There is one other purpose to this book—that is to bring
to those outside economics some helpful and interesting
information about liberal policy. We are, all of us, objects
of policy because we are all affected by it. But we may also
participate in the making of it. Knowing something about
one of the great systems of policy will help us to understand what is happening and what choices are before us.
This knowledge will not tell us what to think and do now.
But it will tell us what once was thought and done.
Whether the ideas described here are relevant today or
whether they are only of historical interest is something
for the present to decide. In making the decision, it will do
well to compare its convictions with those of the past. It
will find, I believe, that liberalism in the meaning given to
it here has a history that is by no means over.

These studies have occupied me for a long while, and from
time to time I have published parts of them as journal articles. This book, however, was planned as a group of
studies about a single idea, and each study was written
as a chapter of the whole. Some of the chapters were then
rewritten and shortened in order to be suitable for journal
publication. That is so of the first four chapters; the last
two have not appeared before in any form. What is presented here represents my considered view of the subject.
It is on some points identical with what it was when the
articles were published, while on other points it is rather
different. I wish to thank the editor of *Ethics* (University
of Chicago Press) for permission to use in Chapter 1 of
Volume I parts of my article entitled "The Moral Hero and
the Economic Man" (Vol. LXI, No. 2, Jan. 1951, pp. 136-
150); the editor of *The Quarterly Journal of Economics*
(Harvard University Press) for permission to use in Chapter
2 of the same volume parts of my article "The Liberal Elements in English Mercantilism" (Vol. LXVI, No. 4, Nov.
1952, pp. 465-501), and in Chapter 2 of Volume II parts of

my article "On the Politics of the Classical Economists" (Vol. LXII, No. 5, Nov. 1948, pp. 714-747); and the editor of *The Journal of Political Economy* (Chicago) for permission to use in Chapter 1 of Volume II parts of my article "Adam Smith and the Economic Man" (Vol. LVI, No. 4, Aug. 1948, pp. 315-336).

There are many people with whom I have discussed the subject and these studies and to whom I am grateful for what I have learned. I hesitate to name some without naming all of them, and from such a list there probably would be inadvertent omissions. However I must state my indebtedness to two of my teachers, Donald A. Anthony and Frank H. Knight, who interested me in the history of economics and directed my first studies in it. They cannot be held accountable for the ideas I have acquired since leaving them, but I must acknowledge my debt to them for what they have taught me.

NOTE ON THE CONTENTS

This work has had to be divided into two volumes, each of about fifty thousand words in length. In making the division I have tried to group the studies in a way that reflects the chronology of the subject and at the same time brings together those studies that express a common view. The reader may use each volume separately or the two of them together.

The first volume is about the intellectual origins of economic liberalism and the first applications of the idea to particular problems of national policy in England and America. It has the subtitle, "The Beginnings," and it contains:

1. The Stoic Origins of Liberalism
2. The Mercantilists as Liberals
3. The Origins of American Liberalism

The second volume examines liberalism as it was expressed by the classical school of economics. This volume, subtitled "The Classical View," contains:

1. The Classical Psychology of Liberalism
2. The Political Ideas of the Classical Economists
3. Liberalism in the Great Century

The same foreword appears in both volumes because it is, I feel, a rather indispensable preliminary to the studies whether the two volumes are read separately or together. The notes at the end of each volume contain the works cited in it.

CONTENTS

ECONOMIC
LIBERALISM

THE CLASSICAL VIEW

THE CLASSICAL PSYCHOLOGY
OF LIBERALISM

There are two elements of classic economic liberalism which, I believe, are more to be studied than any others. One is its ideas of economic psychology in both their positive and normative aspects—how people actually behave and how they ought to behave. Much has been written about these questions, so much in fact that the ideas expressed by the economists themselves have been pretty well obscured. The other is its political ideas, and almost nothing has been written of them. It is informative to study both, because they were directly related to the leading question of this book—What did the liberals believe was the proper relationship between the state and the economic conduct of the individual? This chapter is about economic psychology, and the next is about the politics of the classical economists.

I have chosen to explain Smith's ideas of economic psychology rather than those of any other economist because his were the most consequential. Indeed, his idea of the economic man—or what was believed to be his idea—is probably the longest-lived, most durable, and most familiar idea ever expressed by an economist. It also is the most controversial, with the exception of the idea of the "invisible hand," which also comes from Smith. Actually the two are related parts of his conception of economic motivation.

Early in the nineteenth century, there began a reaction against classical economics, including its normative side which is economic liberalism. The opposition has continued,

and Smith's ideas of economic psychology have been criticized repeatedly. The criticism usually has been directed
against one or more of three beliefs Smith is supposed to
have held: that men are invariably rational and seek to
maximize the satisfaction of given economic wants; that in
their effort to acquire wealth they are governed by a
suprahuman power, the natural law or the invisible hand;
and that the consequence of such effort is a quite satisfactory state of affairs, indeed a harmonious natural order.
If Smith actually believed all this, his "economic man"
would have been a mistaken, even a foolish, idea, and moreover one with implications of mischief.

In contrast to the standard critical view, the point of
view here is that Smith described social behavior in a number of different areas, rational conduct being only one of
them; that in his final and most mature work, *The Wealth
of Nations,* he abandoned the doctrine of natural law in
favor of explaining behavior as the outcome of quite secular
motives; and, finally, that he did not believe free economic behavior necessarily produced a desirable social
order. In support of this interpretation, I shall describe the
chronological development of Smith's ideas of social behavior and especially of its economic aspect. This interpretation is based almost entirely on what Smith himself
said in his writings and very little on what others have said
about him. There is not space enough, nor have I the inclination, to contend with his major critics or to quarrel
with their particular conclusions. Most readers are familiar
in a general way with what has been written about Smith
and can if they wish compare this chapter with such
writing. I do wish to make it clear that my objection to the
commentaries is that they are mistaken. I do not object
to them being commentaries. There are purists among the
historians of economic thought who decry all commentaries
—all books about books—and direct the reader straight to
the masterworks themselves, the direction being given in a
book of course.

1 The Theory of Moral Sentiments

In Smith's writings there are three distinct conceptions of
economic psychology—three versions of the economic man
—and they correspond to the development of the idea in
his three major works. The first was *The Theory of Moral
Sentiments,* published in 1759, and there the normative or
moral aspect of psychology was predominant. His last
work was *The Wealth of Nations,* 1776, and in it he
stressed the positive or factual side of psychology. In between came the *Lectures on Justice, Police, Revenue and
Arms* which he delivered about 1763 but never meant to
publish. In his first book, Smith's main interest was the
question of how man distinguishes right from wrong and
how he acts upon that distinction—i.e., *how* do we know
what is moral and *what* makes us behave morally. The
answers are fairly simple. Moral behavior is that which is
approved by someone else who is not committed to our
situation and so can view it objectively. That person is
the impartial spectator. Usually he is a mental construction
that we make in order to get a disinterested view of our
conduct, but we may have an actual person in mind. From
him we learn what *is* moral. He also makes us want to *be*
moral because, according to Smith, each of us wants the
approval of our fellow men. It is an innate desire. The idea
is an interesting version of "other direction" which David
Riesman uses in *The Lonely Crowd* and is just the opposite
of the Stoic moral hero who was completely inner directed.

ECONOMIC MOTIVATION

In this first work, Smith digressed on economic behavior.
He explained why men are acquisitive and why that
motive is beneficial to others. By an ingenious argument,
he traced the motive to both man's sense of beauty and his
capacity for self-deception. In the eternal fitness of things,
men find beauty. Wealth is one of the fit means to the
good life, the life of virtue and wisdom, and therefore a
thing of beauty. It brings men the approval of their morally

enlightened fellows (the impartial spectator). But the approval actually is mistaken, according to Smith, because wealth is not as fit a means to the good life as it appears to others to be. Once a man has acquired wealth, he finds it is trivial beside the "more solid" attainments of wisdom and virtue. The impartial spectator happens to be wrong. Nonetheless, it is his approval, not our own, that we want. We continue to acquire wealth because others think we thereby come nearer to the good life. Every person's wish is to be taken notice of, to be attended to, to be acclaimed. Hence we work to grow rich even after we no longer want riches as much as we want other things. The desire for approval—for a sympathetic response from others —is a stronger motive than the sense of beauty, but it could never be effective if mankind at large was not mistaken. How the economic man might behave under the eye of an impartial spectator who was a rich man is a problem Smith did not write about.

The role of sympathy as an economic motive is perplexing when set against its place in other forms of behavior. Outside the market, a man must feel that he deserves approbation before he can enjoy it. His conscience is stronger than his vanity and hence the appearance of virtue cannot supplant the reality. But on the market, his conscience is less strong than his vanity. He adds to his fortune simply because it gets him the approval of others. The greater is their gullibility, the happier he is. Smith tries to demonstrate that the illusory quality of wealth is providential: it makes, he says, for an abundance of goods and for social peace. Nevertheless his argument has an unfortunate implication: he makes Providence deprive men of their conscience in order that they will not starve or annihilate each other.[1]

To have avoided the implication, Smith would have had to make utility instead of sympathy the decisive motive of economic behavior and he also would have had to maintain that the possession of wealth *is* the good life, or at least one of its prerequisites. But this line of argument would have produced an embarrassment in another direction.

If wealth is a thing of beauty, what of painting, music, poetry, of man's nature, the heavens? To give all such things the same importance in the design of Providence —to make poetry and pinball contribute equally to the good life—is undiscriminating, to say the least. Smith, like most (but not all) sensible men, refused to carry his argument to its logical conclusion. What utilitarianism ultimately and offensively implies is that among experiences there are only quantitative, not qualitative, differences. The point was not abstract but personal for Smith. Throughout his writings he expressed a dislike for rich people—for their arrogance and ostentation—and showed it in his manner when writing about them. The dislike is most apparent in *The Wealth of Nations* but there is enough of it in the *Moral Sentiments,* the *Essays,* and the *Lectures* to indicate it was something he felt always. Why he should have favored an economic system that fosters money-making is one of the questions which every reader of Smith must ask. The answer, I believe, is that he approved of a market economy because on balance it promoted the good life—the life of learning, beauty, personal virtue, and good works. The belief was qualified however, because he also believed that free economic conduct did not always have these effects. When it did not, he opposed such conduct. This is an explanation of the great paradox in Smith's writings: that he should declare himself for a free market and at the same time oppose many of its results.

ECONOMIC MORALITY

In the *Moral Sentiments* the economic man acts only in his own interest (which is to get approval) and with a prodigious waste of effort (because the approval is undeserved). Still his behavior has beneficial effects on others. His desire for approbation is stronger than his acquisitiveness and forces him to uphold justice. The material progress of society is promoted by the very uselessness of his wealth. After satisfying his own material wants—which, Smith implies, are not much greater than those of the poor—he spends the surplus on retainers, servants, and others, whereby a general plenty is diffused through society. He is guided by an "invisible hand" to promote the welfare of others. In this as in other ways Providence shows its benevolence.[2] The famous words "invisible hand" appear first in *The Theory of Moral Sentiments*.

For all of his good works, the economic man does not secure the highest approval. It is given to behavior that is moral for a better reason than necessity and is benevolent by intention, not accident. The economic man is respected for the practice of the middling virtue of prudence, which is below justice and benevolence and just above propriety, the least of the virtues on Smith's ethical scale. As a prudent creature, he lives within his income, is cautious, and follows the path of security, never yields to (never experiences?) the temptation to make and meddle, never seeks preferment. What he does, steadfastly and with clear head, is to add to his estate. His values under scrutiny are of the family cultivated by Poor Richard, except for an inclination to mind his own business.

His accomplishments are commonplace. Still, his position forces him to join knowledge with prudence and to raise both in esteem, and he stands in strong, if uninspired, contrast with the upper classes, who daily experience the conflict between the temptations of wealth and the requirements of wisdom and virtue. Moreover, the behavior of the economic man has vast indirect consequences, not only in providing for those less fortunate than he but in helping to build the kind of an environment in which the virtues higher than prudence can find expression and which together with wisdom are the highest achievements of men. They never could be brought about, Smith believed, in an aristocratic milieu of wealth and power, which was the milieu of his age.

The economic man was in this way given a place in the benevolent design of the universe. Smith's conception disclosed his faith in the gentleness and wisdom of Providence, a faith which he expressed in his reaction to everything he saw about him. He observed that man was inclined to respect power uncritically and to turn away from the problems of those nearest him; but, he continued, this was fortunate because it supported the class distinctions that civil peace required. Here is an engaging sketch of the "political man," truckling before his master and ignoring his fellow servants with whom he might unite and become master himself. There is an Italian proverb that says when the poor give to the rich the devil laughs. Being more religious, the Italians have been less inclined to mistake their desires for divine guidance. Not so the Anglo-Saxons. They see nothing impious in believing that what they want is what Providence actually meant them to have. Moreover, by being gratified that Providence is benevolent they are in effect commending its works, giving it their approval. The optimism of the eighteenth century strikes me as conceit rather than as something simple-minded, fatuous, or Panglossian.

When the moralists of the period moved away from a faith in natural benevolence, as was notably done by Smith, they did not become irreverent or skeptical but modest and realistic. They also became more informative. Consider how uninformative are other of Smith's observations in *The Theory of Moral Sentiments*. Men, he said, usually look more at the consequences of an act than at its intentions, a habit that seems unjust to those whose good will is defeated and unreasonably generous to those whose good works are fortuitous. Yet what would become of society if approval were granted only for intentions, Smith asks, and answers that every court of justice would become an inquisitorial chamber. At another point he observed that estimable men were often afflicted with an excessive delicacy of sentiment, were more practiced in the "amiable" than in the "manly" virtues, and were unreasonably disturbed by an unjust reproach. Their weakness, however, made the good and the wise indulgent of the failings of others while making them exacting of themselves.

THE MEANING OF NATURAL ORDER

These are features of the natural order which to Smith was the manifestation of the natural law governing social behavior. This order has a much different meaning from the harmony described in *The Wealth of Nations*. According to the doctrine of natural law, averred by Smith in his early writings, and only there, man is endowed with certain characteristics or moral faculties which in their totality comprise human nature. This nature is common to all men in all places and is governed by a force superior to them. That force is the natural law and it emanates from God. The end is beneficent—the glorification of God as his benevolence is revealed in the happiness of man—and the end is realized when the natural order is established. It is inevitable, and in the movement towards it, nature follows a uniform succession of events. Natural law and that which it creates and governs—human nature and natural order— are discoverable by man through the use of his moral faculties. They show him the path of virtue and guide him along it. The philosopher's quest, Smith declared in one of his *Essays,* is to discover the law of nature, to apprehend

> the idea of an universal mind, of a God of all, who originally formed the whole, and who governs the whole by general laws, directed to the conservation and prosperity of the whole, without regard to that of any private individual. . . .[3]

What he meant by this idea, he explained in *The Theory of Moral Sentiments*.

In its economic aspects the idea is not satisfactory, but its defects are inseparable from its merits. The economic man of that book is not helpful in explaining even the main features of economic procedure. He never encounters the problem of economizing because he lives in a world of abundance. If he is successful in acquiring wealth, he also acquires approbation; if not, he is kept from want by the generosity of those who are successful. Having no economic choices to make, the quality of his rational powers is not at issue. If the economic man seeks to maximize anything, it is the approval of the impartial spectator. His choices are moral. He must select the kinds of conduct that will bring him into accord with the natural law. But even that conduct does not necessarily imply rationality. On man's use of reason, Smith is equivocal. He prefers not to say whether men do good because they are reasonable, or because of original instinct, or "some other principle of nature." He only states that man possesses moral faculties and is aware of their exercise by the pleasurable feeling that approbation gives. As long as Smith attended only to these kinds of choices, he could not make a plausible or useful explanation of economic activity. When however his interest in natural law subsided and he came to look at society in a secular and critical way, he then began his contributions to economic thought.

2 *The* Lectures

There are intimations of a new view in the *Lectures on Justice, Police, Revenue and Arms* that were delivered at the University of Glasgow about the year 1763. Its major difference with *The Theory of Moral Sentiments* is in making natural rights instead of natural law the governing principle of society. (The idea later was expressed in detail in *The Wealth of Nations.*) Another and closely related difference is that in the *Lectures* Smith made environment instead of sympathy the force that restrains self-interest. The economic man as a sensitive creature who pursues beauty in a world of material abundance is succeeded by a pedestrian individual who looks with interest upon only those activities which "pay" and pursues luxuries in a society where they are unmistakably scarce.

NATURAL RIGHTS AND ECONOMIC BEHAVIOR

The economic man of the *Lectures,* like his predecessor, still is the best judge of his own interests, he is influenced by what he takes to be the feelings of others toward him, and he has a taste for beauty (although it is frail and fleeting). But here their similarities end. The economic man of the *Lectures,* according to his environment, follows his interest along paths marked out by one or another of two sets of passions. One consists of the "baser" passions of avarice, the instinct for truck, barter, and exchange, the disposition to specialize his labor. They are the more surely grounded, the least in need of any encouragement for their expression. They are traced back to the willfulness in every individual, to his inclination for persuading, imposing upon, and coercing others. As manifestations of self-interest, they usually are regarded with contempt. Yet in the exercise of such "baseness" men discover the more elevated side of their nature, like the sense of beauty, courage, and generosity. These, the other set of characteristics, are delicate and ephemeral. They require much encouragement before they are brought to light, and when they are they attract much commendation.

The individual should be free to express both kinds. It is his natural right to do so. It also is to the interest of others that he do so. His self-interest then will operate to their advantage as well as his own. From the delicate passions comes man's taste for luxuries; out of it commerce develops, liberty takes hold and is made secure, men are emancipated from superstition and come under the influence of learning and the arts. But the delicacy of man would never have had such consequences if he had not been free to specialize his labor, engage in trade, acquire property—if he had not, in other words, had some economic freedom. Smith believed that one of the achievements of his age was this very freedom. He developed in the *Lectures* a theory of economic change that explained the accumulation of capital and the rise of representative government as the outcome of this freedom. Actually more than a theory of change, it disclosed Smith's deep conviction that liberty was both a value in itself and the most effective means of acquiring other values.

A THEORY OF DEVELOPMENT

Toward his ancestors of the Middle Ages, Smith looked with feelings of compassion and also of reproof, frowning upon their waste of time, effort, and wealth; shocked by their depraved pastimes, their callous attitude toward the poor and weak, appalled by their superstition; yet at the same time tolerating their vices in the belief that the

environment permitted nothing better. In that period, the
more elevated side of human nature could not develop.
The inequalities of ownership and opportunity, the restrictions placed upon exchange, the primitive form of agriculture, and the contempt with which most economic activity
was regarded—all turned man's baser instincts away from
those activities which in time would supply him with the
means of indulging his finer nature. His animal spirits, not
to be denied, found an outlet in oppressing the weak and
in making war against the strong. But eventually his avarice broke down the obstacles to exchange and he then was
able to turn his efforts to providing more than the necessi-
ties of life. With the appearance of "luxuries" (which
Smith called all those goods beyond what are required for
a bare subsistence), the aristocracy found a new use for
its income and turned out its retainers, servants, and other
dependents. When Smith wrote *The Wealth of Nations* he
enlarged upon this view of the decline of feudalism and related disdainfully how the aristocracy had squandered its
birthright for trinkets and baubles. It finally was forced to
turn to commerce out of a "principle of avarice" and in so
doing struck away the final restraint on enterprise—the dis-
esteem with which it had been regarded by the ruling
class. Meanwhile those who had been dependent upon the
nobility were forced into productive occupations, and their
characters improved remarkably. Once slothful because
they did not have to work, demeaning before their patrons
and insolent to inferiors, depraved in their tastes and
amusements, they now became industrious, prudent, hon-
est, and enterprising. The transformation of the economy
and of social standards brought with it the development
of representative political institutions. As opportunities
grew for accumulating wealth, men demanded security and
the rule of law: the protection of every man in his person and his property, and the opportunity to trade and
acquire wealth. As men became materially more secure
they were able to look beyond their immediate affairs and
to devote themselves to learning and the arts, to throw off
superstition, and to pursue virtue.

These ideas are what today would be called a theory of economic development and in the past was called a theory of progress. They can be compared instructively with today's theory. Smith's explanation of how a market economy came into being is a piece of speculative history, a statement of how it *could* have originated, not of how it *did* in fact originate. Smith meant his theory to be the latter and cited some facts to support it. But they only illustrate it. The practice of mistaking illustrative for demonstrative evidence is common among historians who present great and inclusive generalizations to explain historical change. The failing is a part of a more basic—and actually a rather simple—error, which is to suppose that because something could have happened in a certain way it must have happened that way, especially if there is no conflicting evidence or recognition of any. About the reasons for the development of capitalism there is a great deal of conflicting evidence, so much that any conjecture like Smith's is unsatisfactory.

What can be said of today's theories of how an industrial system can develop in a backward country? An industrial system is not, to be sure, identical with a market economy. But that is immaterial, because what we want to compare is the *method* of today's economists with that of Smith (not today's *explanation* of the origins of capitalism with that of Smith). Except for the area studies made today, which often are quite empirical, the doctrine of development in its conceptual aspect does not have much more empirical foundation than Smith's theory had. Today's doctrine is mainly deductive, consisting of models of development that are made of propositions from micro- and macro-economics relevant to conditions in which per capita output is rising or can be made to rise. The propositions are logical statements, describing what could happen, not what probably will happen.

What is even more interesting is to compare the two doctrines in their normative aspect. *Why* should a country develop? Modern economists said originally that development is a necessary and probably a sufficient condition for democratic government. More recently they have said development is a necessary condition of political stability, and political stability is prudently left undefined. Some to be sure do say that political stability will be conducive to world peace, and others that development will keep a country independent of the Communist bloc (or blocs).

The view of Smith is, by comparison, a grand vista, a panoramic conception that includes economics, politics, morality, knowledge, and the arts. He believed in development because he believed it to be a condition for political progress, for an improvement in other social relations, for elevating the moral quality of a country, for progress in knowledge and in the arts. In short, he believed an increase in income made the good life possible.

What is most often criticized in Smith's theory of development is the assumption that self-interest will operate beneficently when it is expressed in a free market. If the theory seems simple-minded, one must recall that Smith here was engaged partly in a polemic against restrictions on commerce and partly in expressing his optimistic convictions. When it is summarized so briefly, many of the insights are glossed over, and the rich lesson it held for future generations is discernible only by implication. If any one aspect is to be singled out for emphasis, it is Smith's belief in the power of free economic behavior to produce free, enlightened men. (That this power was not always used wisely Smith was fully aware.) Nothing corrupts an individual so much, he said, as to make him dependent on others for a livelihood and security, and nothing more increases his self-reliance than the opportunity to find his own way in the freedom afforded by equal laws.

There was nothing new in the idea that material dependence is debasing. Vauvenargues said as much in his epigram, "Servitude degrades men even to making them love it." It was a current coin of eighteenth-century thought. So was the apothegm, "He who controls a man's subsistence controls his will." But it was Smith who first emphasized that only through a free market could men emancipate themselves from dependency. Not even Hume, to whom Smith credits the idea, showed so clearly and in such detail the relationship between economic and political freedom. The political institutions of a country are not to be explained, Smith said, by the nature of the governed. That is much the same everywhere. If a Frenchman acts differently from an Englishman, the reason is that the self-interest implanted equally in them finds expression in different economic orders.

In the *Lectures* Smith regarded free government as the product or effect of the free market, not the other way around. Government had important work to do, and that was to protect the free institutions that the free market had brought into being; but it was a passive or protective agency, not one that initiated improvement. This conception departs considerably from Smith's earlier belief that government exists because men find pleasure in submitting to authority; in the *Lectures,* the penchant for authority is merely mentioned and no more. There, the excellence of a government is to be measured by the protection it gives to the natural rights of the individual, and a government which does not provide such protection should be overthrown.

ECONOMIC MORALITY

Not everyone took so favorable a view of the free market as Smith did. He knew that very well. As if in anticipation of what has become a common objection to laisser faire, or to settle with himself the conflicts between the *Lectures* and *The Theory of Moral Sentiments,* he examined the question of justice in relation to economic activity. The economic man of the *Lectures* is virtuous simply because he believes virtue pays. His acquisitiveness is restrained not by the desire for moral approbation but by a disinterested calculation of the returns to be expected from moral as compared with immoral conduct. The calculation shows that on balance there is a net in favor of virtue. By transferring the origin of virtue from man's moral sentiments to his profit and loss statement, Smith worked a very great change indeed in ethical doctrine. Nevertheless he did not touch the reality of virtue itself, nor did he question the comforting notion that whatever prompts men to action the action itself can only be beneficial.

How an individual would act if the calculation by some perverse stroke went in favor of immorality is a troublesome question. And Smith did not evade it. In fact, his willingness to consider the problem of monopoly suggests he was aware of the question. In a monopolistic market, the economic man is not restrained by the rule that honesty equals profitability. By acquiring exclusive privileges of sale or purchase, he can turn dishonesty to a profit, and by carefully managing his power he can so far reduce the menace of potential competitors and outraged customers that his dishonesty can be capitalized for an indefinite period. Smith's solution to the problem was not convincing. He seemed to think that potential monopolists would behave themselves once they realized that monopoly is a game everyone can play and one that in the long run produces losses all around. Neither of these observations happens to be true but they were as much as Smith had to offer in the *Lectures*. In *The Wealth of Nations,* however, there is much more.

An unsure sense of justice is not the only weakness of a free economy. For all of its material, political, moral, and cultural superiority over early forms of economic organization, it was not ideal. The specialization upon which it is based produces a number of undesirable effects, Smith said. The upper classes become preoccupied with acquiring wealth or exhibiting it and they lose sight of the end it should serve: the development of moral and intellectual excellence. They neglect their responsibilities to others, being particularly remiss in the military arts. He took the neglect of military duty to be serious because he believed national defense and power were more important than wealth. The rich are remiss about other responsibilities, and their greatest failing is to become so attached to their wealth that it becomes their sole mark of distinction. In the ostentatious use of wealth Smith saw what was to him perhaps the most unbecoming side of self-seeking. He re-

marked on it in almost all of his writings, and nowhere
more expressly than in an essay on the *Imitative Arts:*

> In arts which address themselves, not to the prudent and the
> wise, but to the rich and the great, to the proud and the vain,
> we ought not to wonder if the appearance of great expence, of
> being what few people can purchase, of being one of the surest
> characteristics of great fortune, should often stand in the place
> of exquisite beauty, and contribute equally to recommend their
> productions.[4]

The quotation is also interesting because it contains the
idea of conspicuous consumption and, what is close to it
but not identical, the idea of commodities as status sym-
bols.

The lower classes also are injured by specialization. Although it improves their living conditions, it also confines
their views and blunts their imaginations, turning them to
vulgar diversions, leaving them witless and without spirit.
By making the employment of children profitable, it puts
obstacles in the way of education and weakens the family.
The neglect of education leaves the great mass of the people insensible to the more creative forms of leisure and
abandons them to the alehouse. So he argued.

It is instructive to contrast Smith's attitude toward the
working class with that of the mercantilists, which is described in the other volume. Smith deplored the condition
of the workers, regretted their weakness before the greater
power of businessmen, hoped that in some way the development of the market would make them richer, freer, wiser,
and more virtuous. He expressed his good will toward the
poor and weak in the warmest, most generous language.
He could find something admirable even in the most lowly,
as when he found the coal heavers to be superb specimens
of manhood and when he observed that the Irish prosti-
tutes of London were the most beautiful women, "perhaps," in the British empire. The mercantilists, on the other
hand, were constantly at the workers, admonishing them,
rebuking, scolding, wheedling, cajoling, punishing, and
preaching virtues of the early-to-bed, early-to-rise variety.

They showed they had very little of the tolerance and generosity expressed by Smith. Yet it was the mercantilists who came forward with explicit and practical proposals for improving the condition of the workers. Whatever one may think of the proposals, either by the standards of their own time or by ours, one must acknowledge that they were an effort to improve the condition of the poor. Indeed, the very harshness that is so repellent today was an indication that the mercantilists cared about the working class (in the same way a stern parent cares about his children). One does not scold and want to improve those to whom one is indifferent. Nor does one urge diligence, enterprise, and self-reliance upon those whom one wishes to become obedient servants of an all-powerful state (which is a common misinterpretation of the mercantilists' views of the laboring classes).

Smith, for his part, did not go much beyond expressing a generous attitude toward the poor. They had his good will in abundance and little more. He did not offer any particular advice about how they could better their condition, either by their own efforts or with the assistance of the state, except to imply that progressive taxation would be desirable. His strongest proposal was to increase the wealth of the nation. When that happened, everyone— the lowly along with the middling and the great—would improve his position. An interesting question is why he did not have practical proposals for helping the poor. The answer may seem to be that he adhered to laisser faire and hence was opposed to trade unions or the regulation of labor markets by the state. But that will not do, because in fact he did not adhere strictly to laisser faire, as this chapter explains farther along. His successors in the nineteenth century were most of them in favor of repealing the prohibition against union organization (the Combination Acts). That does not make them advocates of unions, but does indicate they believed the workers should have the right to form them.

Another direction in which Smith's sympathies lay is disclosed in his frequent comparisons of merchants and manufacturers with the landed gentry. By the time he wrote *The Wealth of Nations* he had no fondness for businessmen, but he still believed their avarice could be turned to public advantage with no great injury to private liberty. He thought quite otherwise of the landholders. He believed their interests were in direct conflict with those of workers and businessmen. When one compares what he wrote about businessmen and land owners, one can see that he considered the businessman more useful to the nation. His attitude was unusual for the age. To claim that a merchant and manufacturer were entitled even to as much esteem as a landholder was uncommon. To claim they were entitled to more—because they were superior in prudence, energy, social usefulness, learning, and morality—was notable.

NATURAL RIGHTS VERSUS NATURAL LAW

Smith noted some major failings of a free market when he gave the *Lectures* and many more of them in *The Wealth of Nations*. Nevertheless he has been described repeatedly as the great apologist for laisser faire. His doctrine is said to rest on a faith in a natural order in economic affairs. Actually the idea of nature appears only remotely in the *Lectures*. Its hand is more than invisible; it is unpredictable and capricious. One of the two distinctive features of the *Lectures*, which marks it off from *The Theory of Moral Sentiments*, is the ambiguity surrounding the idea of natural law. The other is the appearance of the idea of natural rights. Smith refers to the natural right of each person to his life and to security against violence, the natural right of inheritance, and the natural right to private property. He refers also to the political analogues of these rights, the most important of which is the natural right of each man to associate with others on terms agreeable to all of them. As Smith uses the term, a natural right is the liberty each man should have to act in a way that is consistent with his inclinations, to some of which he is disposed by psychological traits and to others by choice. The belief that each man possesses undeniable rights necessarily implies that he must respect the rights of others. It also implies that all men together must so arrange their social behavior that each may have what is due him. Since man is psychologically disposed to specialize his economic effort, he has a right to exchange his product for that produced by the specialized effort of others. It follows that there can be no legitimate interference with exchange, either by private persons or by public bodies. In the property which a man acquires by his activity he has a natural right, and when the property passes to his heirs they too have a natural right in it. Because the free exercise of individual inclinations depends most fundamentally on personal security, the right of each man to his life is the primary natural right. Any interference with the free expression of individual desires is a deprival of natural rights. Any serious attempt to stifle them is therefore a signal for justifiable if not obligatory resistance. In liberal philosophy from Hooker onward, the greatest menace to freedom was thought to dwell in the state, or in those agencies like monopolies that Smith thought derived their power from the state.

Just where natural rights originate is not made clear. There is evidence that they simply are the data of social behavior. All of man's traits and desires when taken together exhibit a harmonious design. All fall into one of two categories of "passions" which serve to reinforce and complement one another. Smith gave the *Lectures* not many years after *The Theory of Moral Sentiments* was published and he may still have thought of nature as incorporating mankind in its harmonious design. Whatever is the origin of the "passions," they are not, in the *Lectures,* governed by nature. They may be its work but no longer are its "darling charge." Many of the *Lectures* are taken up with showing how natural characteristics are stifled or distorted, with showing the difficulties encountered by self-interest, and with the reforms that should be made in order that man can be free to express himself. If Smith had really believed (as he has been said to have believed) that the will of nature inevitably is realized, there would have been no reason for him to condemn the effort to obstruct it and no reason for him to suggest ways in which its work could be made easier.

THE NATURAL ORDER AS COMPETITION

A more plausible interpretation is that Smith gave a secular explanation of human behavior, not one derived from natural, or suprahuman law. The *Lectures* say that the way men behave depends on their environment and that human nature is governed by the interaction between the individual and society. In this idea there are the beginnings of a new conception of natural order. Natural order is no longer the expression of divine will. It now is the kind of social organization that develops when men can use their traits in their own interest. The conception is radically different from that in *The Theory of Moral Sentiments* where the natural order is the outcome of man's bringing his moral sentiments into accord with God's will. The world that results has no economic problems because it experiences no scarcity. The concern Smith shows in the *Lectures* for the protection of natural rights connotes a new conception of economic behavior. He no longer believed in natural abundance. He did say that if man wanted no more than subsistence he never would engage in economic activity. But he does want more. To get it he utilizes his talents for specialization and exchange, thereby obtaining a greater satisfaction than he would acquire by producing for his own use. In this idea is the suggestion that the meaning of economic behavior is the maximizing of returns from scarce means.

The effective use of talents is not, however, realized only by specialization and exchange. It depends also on the conditions of exchange. In order to satisfy wants most effectively, the products of specialized effort must be exchanged on a free market. For this reason, Smith condemned monopolies and restrictions on international trade. With disarming candor, he asked, "Unless we use the produce of our industry, unless we can subsist more people in a better way, what avails it?" [5]

From these considerations of the role of natural law and natural characteristics in the *Lectures,* one can infer that the natural order is the competitive market. The natural order has little or no relation to a purposive nature disposing and ordering the social relations among individuals. It is ideal, not because it reveals the design of nature but because competition is the most practicable (thus, "ideal") method of protecting the natural rights of individuals and of providing the greatest possible wealth to the nation. Stated in a somewhat different way, competition is the ideal instrument for securing freedom as a value in itself and as an effective means to other values.

3 The Wealth of Nations

In *The Wealth of Nations* Smith developed in detail the idea of natural order. There the natural order is offered as the ideal organization of society. That is because it represents man's greatest opportunity to realize his desire for freedom and his best effort to utilize for himself and for society his natural endowments. It is *not* ideal in being the handiwork of nature, because in fact nature has little to do with its origin or being. If this natural order was offered by Smith as the best of all possible worlds, as some critics have contended, it must be understood to be no different from the least undesirable of worlds. In it Smith placed the third economic man to appear in his writings. The behavior of individuals is brought into harmony by competition. But now competition is not the exclusive instrument of control, and the exceptions taken to it are numerous and substantial. Smith in *The Wealth of Nations* is conditional in his judgment, skeptical, and sometimes sardonic. He imputes no natural goodness to men. He implies that if anything is natural it is more than a little ignobility. Their behavior is made harmonious by a process of mutual negation. The evil they wish and do injures no one but themselves, and the vast energies which their self-seeking releases are turned to the nation's advantage. The essential difference between this natural order and that described in *The Theory of Moral Sentiments* is in the conception of justice. Justice is no longer regarded as the charge of a benevolent deity but as the particular care of government which exists for the very mundane reason of protecting property.

AVARICE, INDOLENCE, AND ECONOMIZING

The economic man of Smith's last work differs from his predecessors of the other two works by the very great power of his material self-interest. He is driven relentlessly to improve his material condition, there being scarcely an instant of his life when he is not looking about for ways of adding to his fortune. Smith is extravagant in emphasizing this interest. In one passage he makes government and law crumble before it; in another, it is a universal trait uniting all men of all lands in a common humanity of self-seeking; in still another, it is a biological fact independent of environment and transmitted through successive generations by heredity, as when he writes that the desire to better our condition comes with us at birth. These passages have formed the conventional impression of the economic man. It was summarized by one of the more entertaining of the critics of classical economics, Thomas Love Peacock, in *Crochet Castle,* where the formidable Rev. Dr. Folliott is made to say:

My principles, sir, in these things are, to take as much as I can get, and to pay no more than I can help. These are everyman's principles, whether they be the right principles or no. There, sir, is political economy in a nutshell.

Despite the connotations of Smith's statements, self-interest is not directed only to material ends. An individual may find his interest in coddling his vanity; in exercising a natural desire to deceive and impose upon others and a just as natural desire to be gulled himself; in upholding his social position; in furthering animosity against his fellows; in supporting prejudices even more mischievous against foreigners; or simply in indulging his indolence. Indeed, the economic man may turn his efforts away from acquiring wealth and toward satisfying any inclination that may strike him. But among all of his desires there is no desire to be just and benevolent—an omission which can hardly pass unnoticed in view of the cardinal place these virtues have in *The Theory of Moral Sentiments*. In *The Wealth of Nations* the personality traits of individuals motivate their economic conduct; the motivation is not, as in *The Theory of Moral Sentiments,* a moral sense. One instructively can examine the relationship between the trait of indolence and that of pecuniary self-interest, because the relationship tells us much about Smith's final conception of economic psychology (namely, that expressed in *The Wealth of Nations*). Smith said men love their ease and find labor to be painful. That is different from his saying men are driven into pursuing wealth—different but not inconsistent. Between the desire for wealth and the desire for a life of ease, the former is the stronger. But avarice does not eliminate indolence, rather is conditioned by it. Men look for ways of minimizing the effort necessary for acquiring wealth. They are, therefore, confronted with the problem of using scarce means to achieve unlimited ends. The economic man is a great respecter of the maxim, It is better to play for nothing than to work for nothing—a maxim, one may remark, that expresses the psychological disposition at the basis of the labor theory of value and all "pain cost" doctrines. The psychological setting in which Smith placed the economic problem does not make the problem any more real. Even if men were not indolent, they still would wish to use their time as efficiently as possible. But a characteristic of the age in which Smith wrote was to trace all problems back to the data of human nature.

Out of the relationship between avarice and indolence Smith developed his view of economic behavior, calling on certain other traits as the occasion required. In the interest of efficiency, men specialize their efforts and engage in exchange. Specialization enables an individual to impose on others a portion of the disagreeable labor which is inseparable from the pursuit of wealth. Far from scrupling to impose on others, he is led to it naturally. The economic man values his specialized talents in proportion to the amount of toil they enable him to escape and to shift upon others. He values his own product not by the labor it cost him but by the labor he would have to expend if he were to produce himself what he obtains in exchange. The labor he would have to use to produce what he buys is always greater (certainly never is less) than the labor he uses to produce what he sells. Viewing labor effort in this subjective way is perhaps a clue to the ambiguity in the more technical aspect of Smith's theory of economic value. The view makes clear some of the statements in the first book of *The Wealth of Nations* where "labor command" and "labor quantity" are used interchangeably. Others, unfortunately, resist this interpretation.

The belief that man is naturally inclined to impose on others is of more significance, however, in suggesting a different view of economic motivation than for the light it may throw on the labor theory of value. This inclination can be taken as something that supports specialization and in other ways promotes economic activity, or it can be taken as a disposition that finds a reward in its own exercise. Smith occasionally verged on saying that men engage in specialization because it is an outlet for their egoism, which is to say that labor is its own gratification and not a means to something else. It cannot then be painful—unless individuals are afflicted with some sort of perversity which drives them to make life unpleasant for themselves or for others. Though Smith was skeptical of the quality of human motives, he seems not to have been interested in ferreting out perversity. His suggestion that the market is governed by egoism is significant for anticipating the modern notion that economic activity can be its own reward, that it often has the character of a game played more for its intrinsic interest than for its prize.

Smith, however, did not pursue the idea. He placed specialization predominately at the service of pecuniary desires and he made egoism the ultimate motive of all behavior. He strongly suggested that if men are observed

closely, whether on the market, in politics, in the classroom,
or in casual association, their self-seeking will reveal itself.
Among the lower classes, egoism is necessarily directed toward making a living, and the behavior of the workers is
governed mainly by economic circumstances. Their success
in acquiring the materials of life has much to do with their
moral and intellectual merit. If they escape poverty and
are secure about the future, the masses will turn to the
practice of virtue and wisdom. If, however, they are poor
and uncertain about tomorrow's wage, their need to make
a living will overwhelm all other interests, and any other
activity will be beyond their power. What Smith implied
is that for the greatest part of the population, happiness,
truth, beauty, and goodness depend on real income. This
idea, one should notice, is just the opposite of the idea expressed in his first work that wealth does not bring happiness and that those who pursue it will be disappointed.

Although their behavior is more thoroughly colored by it
and their outlook is wholly dependent on it, the common
people are not alone in being materialistic. The same characteristic is disclosed in men of all classes and nowhere
more certainly than in their political behavior. This is apparent in Smith's remarks on government, the point of
which is that cupidity explains most conduct—or, more ac-
curately, misconduct. When he said that avarice is the occasion for most wrongdoing, he was repeating what his age
took from Cicero, one of its political mentors. Cicero said
that men usually are led to do wrong by their egoism and
that "in this vice, avarice is generally the controlling motive." [6]

Notably missing from *The Wealth of Nations* is the in-
genuous psychological explanation of sovereignty which
is in *The Theory of Moral Sentiments* and is intimated in
the *Lectures*. In its place, there is a theory of government
which at times is materialistic enough for an economic de-
terminist. The pathetic political man of Smith's first work
is pushed aside by a calculating individual who respects
the authority of government because it protects his wealth
—or because he thinks it does. Although he agrees to re-

spect the property rights of everyone, especially those who are richer than he, he does so only because he fears that disrespect for authority will expose him to the cupidity of those beneath him.

> No thing in use by man, for power or ill,
> Can equal money. This lays cities low,
> This drives men forth from quiet dwelling-place,
> This warps and changes minds of worthiest stamp,
> To turn to deeds of baseness, teaching men
> All shifts of cunning . . .

These lines of Sophocles express the idea that was a starting point for most of the political speculation of the seventeenth and eighteenth centuries. The Enlightenment infused the idea with a faith in the capacity of men to know that their long-range interests required them to respect authority and to know that these interests were more likely to have a satisfactory outcome in an environment governed by the free market.

SELF-INTEREST AND DISHARMONY

When Smith passed from discussing social activity in the large to examining its minutiae, he again stressed the power of the pecuniary interest and was quite frank in noting that it frequently had undesirable consequences. Because the remuneration of lawyers and their clerks was proportioned to the length of the documents they prepared, they so extended them as to confound the language of the law. Since university professors received a guaranteed stipend, they were lax in their instruction, and education fell into a wretched state. Wealthy families of the time engaged traveling tutors for their sons—than which nothing could be worse for both tutor and pupil, Smith declared (possibly out of experience because he had been a traveling tutor). But to allow the pecuniary interest to operate among the clergy would produce a particularly odious form of competition, because if the income of a clergyman were to depend on the size of his congregation the advantage would go to those who played on the superstition of their charges, leaving religion to suffer and zealotry to flourish. About the value of competitive behavior in the professions, Smith was pragmatic. In certain instances, such as education, he felt that pecuniary sanctions had been too far removed, while in others he was opposed to applying them—at least to applying them as strongly as in the market for ordinary goods and services.

But Smith did more than question the social merit of the desire for gain. In the passages that were not expressly about economic policy he often questioned the power of the desire and occasionally its very reality. There are few chapters in *The Wealth of Nations* which do not in some way qualify the idea that the acquisitive instinct is relentless and invincible. The economic man is much affected by his environment and most liable to passing fancies. He is, Smith observed, a very vain creature. Although vanity is an expression of egoism it does not lead him to a successful maximizing of economic values. Indeed, it often defeats the pecuniary interest, turning men away from prudent investment to an ostentatious use of wealth. They carry their pride to the market place and take absurd risks with their fortunes. Smith observed that a common failing, not only of the vain but of every person in tolerable health and good spirits, was to overestimate the chance of gain, to regard himself a favorite of fortune. Sometimes, however, conceit is restrained by the desire for security, especially after a few spectacular failures have chastened an individual's conceit. He then may be averse to taking even a reasonable risk. In addition, there are other traits which stifle or divert the operation of the pecuniary interest, such as irrationality, error, ignorance, indolence, and inertia. All of them turn an individual away from the most economic use of his talents and occasionally from gratifying any desire whatever. Of the many examples which Smith provides, two may be cited. A merchant may so avidly desire to monopolize the market that he fails to anticipate the monopolistic behavior of others, and all may find their avarice disappointed. Individual workers do not always seek out the market in which the highest wages are paid, because they may be ignorant of alternative opportunities or they may be held to their jobs by sheer inertia.

The environment of an individual as well as his distinctive psychological traits modifies the expression of the acquisitive instinct. Smith stated again in *The Wealth of Nations* that the form in which agricultural land was held during the Middle Ages impeded economic progress and the accumulation of capital. He observed that social custom casts some occupations into disrepute and makes for differences in wages and profits—differences which could not exist in an impersonally perfect market. Finally, the form of government and the character of the laws interfere with the maximization of returns, this influence being shown most clearly in national animosity against foreigners and unavoidably in the requirements of national power.

One can easily cite many more instances in which the pecuniary interest fails to operate perfectly or does not operate at all. These however should be sufficient to show that the economic man of *The Wealth of Nations* was not the creature he is reputed to be. Indeed, in those passages where Smith is not exposing the futility of political efforts to restrict the pecuniary interest he is as often as not explaining that the interest either operates imperfectly or to the disadvantage of society. The "uniform, constant, uninterrupted effort of every man to better his own condition" is in fact not uniform, is inconstant, and frequently interrupted; the acquisitive instinct which "comes with us from the womb, and never leaves us till we go into the grave" is really not that basic at all.

When Smith wrote of the great power of material self-interest, what he probably meant to do was to describe a tendency of behavior; and when he said this interest was beneficent, he probably meant that to control it was risky. The beneficence in fact depends mainly on environment. He observed that if obstacles were placed in the way of the pecuniary interest there would result a great waste of resources. That, he believed, had happened in the medieval era. Because men had little opportunity of turning their efforts to profit, they were indolent. The resulting economic loss was a misfortune, and so too was the kind of moral atmosphere that indolence and dependence breeds. In writing of his own age, Smith implied that its superiority lay in the measure to which the pecuniary interest was given a wider area of freedom and operated under more equitable laws. Freedom brought an increase in the wealth of the nation, and with the general plenty that ensued there was, he felt, an elevation of moral and intellectual standards.

Nevertheless he did not offer his age as a model. It was neither ideal nor the best to be had. This conclusion is implied in his strictures against the economic behavior of his times and in those remarks in which he intimates his conception of the ideal as opposed to the economic man. Where Smith's age failed to achieve all within its power, its failure was the result of stifling the pecuniary interest or of allowing it to operate unequally. Hence, his condemnation of political attempts to control the "industry" of individuals; his excoriation of monopoly, as a denial of the equality of a competitive market; his clearly evinced sympathies for the poor as victims of the inequitable effects of "industry," and his implied proposals for something resembling progressive taxation.[7] These criticisms were the negative side of his conviction that the free market is the best possible method of organizing—and controlling—economic activity. If there is a free market, the expression of the pecuniary motive *usually* produces a desirable effect. However, if the market is not free the result may be outrageous, and the only remedy for too little freedom may be even less of it. If, for example, society is so unfortunate as to practice slavery and is averse to abolishing it, Smith suggests that the proper policy is for the government to interfere with the free use of property rather than to look on indifferently while the master treats the slaves as he pleases. The faith in a benign arrangement of social relations, which is manifested unequivocally in *The Theory of Moral Sentiments* and often ascribed to Smith's last work as well, is disclosed in *The Wealth of Nations* only in the belief that economic freedom can produce a harmonious (i.e. acceptable) social order. Although far from ideal, the order is the best within man's limited capacity.

But man's poor powers left Smith restive. In going over the more critical passages of *The Wealth of Nations*, one feels that Smith's private ideal was different from what he urged on the world. He was dismayed by much economic behavior even when it was competitive. He reiterated in his last work all of those deficiencies of the enterprise economy which he had put down in the *Lectures:* the feeble sense of justice, the disregard for wisdom, the flamboyant use of wealth, the indifference to social responsibility, the dispirited outlook of the lower classes. The good life, according to Smith, seems to have meant the performance of good works and the cultivation of knowledge. His aversion to the habits of businessmen had become so pronounced in his final work as to leave little doubt that however practicable he thought competition to be, he did not thereby approve of the psychological traits that produced it. "Of the money-making that depends on troublesome going about and seeing people and doing business" he had little use, no more than Plutarch ascribes to the Spartans under Lycurgus. If there is a common theme running through all of Smith's works, it is an underlying disquietude with the moral and intellectual tenor of a commercial society. In view of the uses to which *The Wealth of Nations* has been put and of the place it gave Smith in history, this is paradoxical. The philosopher who did more than anyone to justify the ways of the free economic man found him personally distasteful.

THE COMPETITIVE HAND

The natural order which is the achievement of the economic man is a system that on examination turns out to be almost identical with the conception of perfect competition in modern price theory. Exchange to be effective must be impersonal, Smith stated in demonstrating the folly of bilateral trade. There must be mobility of factors of production and a free movement of goods between regions and countries. Buyers and sellers must know the conditions

of the market in order for their activity to have the most desirable effect. Finally, there must be many buyers and
sellers.[8] All that is missing, as a student of price theory will
notice, is a homogeneous product.

Competition is possible only in the presence of certain
political conditions. In prescribing them Smith was decid-
edly negative. Laws must be established to make property
secure, including the property each man has in his own
labor, and security calls for an exact and equal administra-
tion of justice. The political reforms for which Smith asked
did not call for the passage of as much new legislation as
of the repeal of old, such as the laws supporting monopolies, the tariff and other restrictions on international trade,
and the ill-conceived efforts of the state to regulate production and consumption. Let the governors look after
their own affairs, and the people can be trusted to look
after theirs—so Smith summarized his negative position.
Actually many of the restrictions he wanted to remove had
been allowed to lapse by the refusal of the courts to enforce them, even though the laws that authorized them had
not been repealed.

It will be observed that the economic and political elements of the natural order are not the work of a divine
power. They are produced by wholly secular forces. The
harmony in this order comes from the mutual advantage of
exchange. The advantage in turn comes from the specialization of labor and the exchange of its product. Specialization makes for an efficient use of resources. It does
so by allowing each individual to cultivate his particular
genius and so obtain maximum efficiency; by permitting
him to produce as much as he pleases and so secure the
disposition between effort and leisure most satisfactory to
himself; and by allowing him to exchange his product for
that of others of dissimilar abilities on terms satisfactory
to all of them. Each man knowing he can exchange his
product for that of others will exert his industry in order
to obtain as much as possible for himself, and with all men
doing this a "general plenty diffuses itself through all the
different ranks of society." This idea is usually criticized

by disputing the contention that the maximizing of individual incomes necessarily maximizes the real income of society. An individual, it is pointed out, may obtain a greater income by restraining his industry than by exerting it. This is of course quite true, but it is not a refutation of Smith's conception of natural harmony. Indeed, it confirms what he had to say. If competition does not rule, the restricting of effort may raise the incomes of monopolists, and that was why Smith opposed them.

The competitive harmonies reveal themselves on the market in the system of relative prices. As consumers, individuals pay the lowest possible prices for what they buy, and producers are able to sell at low prices because of the efficiency that competition forces upon them. The wages of labor rise to their natural level (that which permits the population to maintain itself), because no single employer can force them down. Capital, being free to enter the areas of greatest yield, becomes allocated to the most productive uses. Harmony, it must be repeated, is not produced by any benevolence inherent in individuals, or by the wisdom of government, or by the generous disposition of nature. It is the outcome of the pecuniary interest operating under conditions that make no other outcome possible. The famous invisible hand of *The Wealth of Nations* is nothing more than the automatic equilibration of a competitive market.[9]

There were two sides to Smith's argument for competition. One was that competition serves the material interests of the individual. The other was that competition adds to the power of the state by increasing the national output. Both sides of the argument elucidate his thesis that only through freedom can the welfare of the nation be increased and can individuals realize their natural rights. In this sense did he believe that what was good for the individual was good for society.

He was not, however, optimistic about achieving such a social order. If the entrenched prejudices of the public against competition could be overcome there would remain the more formidable resistance of vested interests, the defeat of which he thought was very unlikely. This alone should dispose of the notion that he believed the competitive order was part of the ineluctable workings of benign nature. Not only was he far removed from such a faith but he was far also from having much confidence in the ability of individuals to know their own welfare. If he was at all optimistic, he was so only in thinking that the economic man, as frail as he was in understanding and frailer still in execution, still knew his interests better than his governors could know them, and in thinking that the economy would be better off if each individual looked after his interests in his own way.

There is still another qualification which must be made to the beneficence of the pecuniary interest. Even when the interest is expressed in a competitive market, it has only a *tendency* to produce a harmonious order. Smith did not say that competition invariably produces the greatest possible wealth and the most desirable distribution of it. (And of course he denied with even greater force that the operation of avarice is desirable in every kind of an environment.) In the most free of markets, individual enterprise will not find the supplying of certain indispensable goods and services to be profitable, and they must be supplied by the state or not at all. Apart from this failing, free enterprise divides the national wealth in a way that is deficient by most standards of distributive justice. Individuals will receive what they are worth on a free market, but the way in which the market values their services and the way in which they *should* be valued will be two very different things if power is unequally distributed.

4 The Achievement of Smith

By relating Smith's views of social behavior to the questions raised in the opening pages of this chapter, one can find four different areas of conduct described in *The Wealth of Nations* and in those parts of the *Lectures* that are most consistent with it. He stated that one part of the behavior of men is like the behavior of all biologic organisms seeking to gratify physical tastes; this area is not described in detail. More important is the behavior of the individual as a psychological mechanism, and throughout Smith's work this behavior receives the greatest emphasis. Man as a self-interested creature is described in great detail. He is proud, vain, willful, indolent, acquisitive, and, in viewing other persons as useful in getting what he wants, he is immoral in the fundamental sense of treating other people as means instead of as ends. As a psychological mechanism he pursues his interest in a way that is governed by his environment, the economic aspect of which interested Smith most. One element in the constitution of the economic man is compounded of these psychological traits. His behavior in this area is purely mechanical, following an invariable pattern of stimulus and response. He observes an opportunity to become richer and unconsciously adopts certain conventional means in order to take advantage of it. His behavior here is not rational; it is more like that of an automaton than that of a calculating creature.

The third area of conduct is that in which the individual deliberates about the best means of achieving certain given ends, such as fortune or fame. Here the economic man ponders the best way of laying out his fortune and talents in order to acquire the largest returns. The returns are not entirely economic and some of them are not economic at all. He may desire prestige, ostentation, power and other marks of social superiority as well as an increase in his wealth, but whatever is the goal he seeks he does not question it. In the fourth area of conduct, the individual deliberates about the objectives which he ought to pursue. The nature of conduct in this area is such that men consider the most suitable use for wealth; they examine ways of best using their freedom and of increasing it. As a result of such deliberation, their environment is consciously changed, and behavior in all other areas, which assumes given means or given ends, or both, is altered.

So much for what Smith *did* believe when he wrote *The Wealth of Nations*. It is instructive to consider what he did *not* say, by way of contrast and also in order to summarize his principal views of human nature and society. (a) He did not say that the economic man was a rational creature who invariably pursues his pecuniary interest and is uniformly successful in realizing it. He may be acquisitive or not, depending on his environment and on other traits and desires; he may be a rational creature or he may be a passive agent, depending on his ability to rise above the level of mechanical behavior. (b) Smith did not say that the economic man was moved by a providential force and was preordained to occupy a harmonious social order. The economic man is governed by human nature, expressing itself in manifold ways, and how it came into being Smith does not say. In view of the salient omission of any reference to natural law as the origin of human nature, one reasonably may assume that human nature is a datum. The natural order of the economic man is the product of his pecuniary interest seeking expression on a free market. The natural order is simply competition. As competition has its origin partly in the psychological constitution of men and partly in their natural rights, it had a more compelling justification than any alternative form of economic organization. (c) The economic man is not benevolently inclined, and the good works which he performs are no part of his intention. Even in the most competitive of markets, the consequences of his acts can be undesirable and require social intervention. (d) Finally, the economic man is not a free agent with the right of producing what he pleases, selling where he pleases, and of doing with his wealth what he pleases. He is subject to the severe discipline of competition and the more formal restraints imposed by law. His freedom of enterprise stops short of the privilege of denying freedom to others.

None of the conceptions of economic behavior offered by Smith in his three major works conforms to the accepted version of the economic man. If any of Smith's abstractions resemble this fiction, it is the economic man of *The Theory of Moral Sentiments,* but even here the resemblance is slight, consisting only in their both being governed by natural law. In Smith's later works, which contain little or no reference to natural law, his conception of economic behavior is radically different. In *The Wealth of Nations* particularly, Smith presented a twofold justification of economic freedom. Reasoning from the doctrine of natural rights, he declared that each man should be free to pursue his material interests in his own way. He also said that the psychological traits of man led him to specialization and exchange. The consequence was a social order in which freedom was respected as a value in itself and as the most effective means to other values. Even though he could not be in sympathy with many of the motives and tastes of the economic man, Smith accepted him in preference to those who previously had dominated society. As rough and imperfect as he was, his vigor held more promise than the behavior of the aristocracy. Smith raised the economic man from the class of pariahs, giving him a new status as well as a new freedom, because in competitive behavior he saw the requisites of cultural progress. He gave a new emphasis to individualism by making free economic behavior a natural right, by asserting that men should be free to seek their own welfare because they were men and were not agents in the hands of an inexorable nature, however benevolent, or of a powerful state, however benign.

2

THE POLITICAL IDEAS
OF THE CLASSICAL
ECONOMISTS

The political ideas of the classical economists have an interesting and a significant relation to their ideas of economic policy. An analysis of the relation uncovers two paradoxes. They are important in themselves and they are important for what they tell us of the development of economic liberalism after the middle of the eighteenth century.

The classicists urged economic freedom on the world and in doing so they were expressly or by implication saying that all men should have the right to seek their material welfare in their own way. This right was "natural" to them in one of two senses or both. It was natural because it was either a psychological characteristic or a political privilege with which they were born, or both. Now to say that each man has a right to make economic choices is to imply that he also has a right to make political choices. I do not mean that a free market, in every argument that can be made for it, necessarily implies a government based on universal consent, i.e., a democracy. A free market can be justified on grounds of efficiency and not of psychology or ethics—as, for example, it could be justified in an authoritarian state as a means of maximizing consumer satisfaction. It need not be justified as a means of permitting people to make choices for the sake of making them, a justification derived from the Stoic conception that virtue consists in the act of choice and not in the thing chosen. The justification given the free market by the classical economists was related to the Stoic conception but was not the same. The economists justified it as a means of allowing the individual to exercise his natural right to make economic choices, and the justification implies he also should have a means of exercising his natural right to make political choices. That implies a democratic form of government and suggests the classical economists should have favored such a government. But they did not.

In the opposition of these views is one paradox: A free market implies what may be called universal economic enfranchisement, but limitations on representative government deny men the political freedom that is the analogue of a free market. This paradox is exactly the opposite of that which usually is attributed to capitalism, namely that capitalism provides political but not economic democracy.

The second paradox is implicit in the opposition between the classical doctrine of free international trade and the belief of the economists in the advantages of a strong national state, a belief manifested in their views on military establishments, on the defense of Britain, and on the relationship of liberty to national power. If all countries traded freely with each other, some commodities that are essential to national power would be produced in only a few countries and not all of them in any one country. Other goods would be produced more widely but not all of them in sufficient quantity to support power. There eventually would come into being a world political condition in which national states, as carriers of decisive power, would be impossible or unlikely. What now are nations would become regional economies, which would be bound together by ties of mutual economic dependence and a common condition of political (or at least military) impotence. This paradox was to succeeding generations a little less evident than the first, but it was more obvious to the classical economists themselves. It was to Smith because he wrote in favor of the Navigation Acts and other measures which increased the national power of Britain but diminished its real income.

In seeking to uncover the source of these paradoxes, I shall refer mainly (although not exclusively) to the writings of Hume and Smith and to the historical circumstances of

which they seemed most aware; because in the early
riod of classicism the paradoxes were most striking. Excep.
for differences in emphasis and detail, what is said here of
Hume and Smith will apply also to most of the other figures in the classical school, like Malthus, James Mill, Ricardo, McCulloch, and Senior. The ideas of John Stuart
Mill are of a quite different sort and are described separately at the close of this chapter.

1 The Political Philosophy of Hume and Smith

The political doctrine of the classical economists was in fact
liberal and consistent with their economic policy, despite
its paradoxical relationship to the idea of a free market.
Their standards of political *practice*—as distinct from *doctrine*—can be described as "utilitarian," as that word is
taken in its ordinary and limited meaning. The political
structure they advocated was a representative government
of a type common in the liberal tradition. In the way they
viewed the objectives of political organization, the economists were in agreement with the political philosophers of
the seventeenth century. The economists departed from
them in certain practical, or utilitarian, matters. The economists gave less emphasis to the methods of government
than to its end; they were less exacting about the organization of the state; and they believed that such matters
were to be appraised by the success of any particular political organization in achieving the primary ends of liberalism. In this sense their standards of political practice were
utilitarian. This latitude did not, however, make them
wholly indifferent to the form of government: although
they looked upon the organization or structure of the state
less critically than upon its intentions and its effects, they
did believe in keeping the structure within the limits of
what Smith called "republicanism."

A SUMMARY STATEMENT

To the eighteenth century, even more than to the liberal
philosophers of the preceding century and a half, govern-

ments were a necessary evil at best and at worst were "engines of despotism." They reflected unhappily on the imperfect constitution of human nature and existed only to serve very limited ends, ends that unfortunately could not be realized by agreement alone but needed a coercive agency. To the classical economists, the primary objective of political organization was the protection and increase of individual liberty, in which was included the liberty to accumulate property. The principal condition for realizing this end was the maintenance of peace and order through government by law. Among the things to be secured, a major item was private property. In establishing social peace as the great desideratum, the economists had in mind something more than merely preserving the status quo. They looked upon political stability as the condition for advancing the more important ends of individual liberty and the free use of wealth. But although they were not committed to the status quo—and were very clear in asserting the right of a people to rebel against authority—neither were they light-minded about revolution. This attitude is made plain by Smith in his *Lectures on Police, Justice, Revenue and Arms,* where, after stating that utility is the foundation of government, he declared that once a government loses its usefulness it no longer has any right to exist and should be overthrown; but, he continued, the people will do well to bear many inconveniences before taking on themselves the responsibility for revolution. These "inconveniences" may be no mere trifles; they may be major violations of individual liberty, to be endured by nothing short of heroic patience. So one may infer from *The Wealth of Nations.* The evils of government and governors are painted very black indeed, but at no point does Smith suggest that revolution is the remedy (as some of his American admirers did).

Although the classical economists wrote less about the form of government than about its objectives and seemed to think it less important, still almost all of them proposed limited representative institutions and an hereditary monarch as a stabilizing agency. Such a government was described in a variety of ways. To Hume, it was an aristocracy; to Smith, a republic; to James Mill, a system of checking bodies; to Nassau W. Senior, a mixed government. These descriptions were hardly more diverse than the party sympathies of the economists. Hume was a Tory while Smith was inclined to the Whigs; James Mill also was a Whig, and Ricardo sided with its radical wing on most of the issues that arose when he was in the House of Commons. But despite the differences in party attachment, the economists were pretty well agreed among themselves on political principles.

This summary statement of their politics seems to place them outside the political philosophy of the Enlightenment as it is stated in such works as Richard Hooker's *The Laws of Ecclesiastical Polity, The Leviathan* of Hobbes, the second *Treatise on Civil Government* of Locke, Montesquieu's *Spirit of the Laws,* and the pragmatism of Halifax (George Savile). These men differ in many ways, but they express some common suppositions about man and society. One is that man is by nature motivated by a desire for material gain and the motive has no natural limits. It leads him to grasp what he can in complete disregard for the rights of others. When expressed in a state of nature—i.e., in the absence of government—it leads men to war upon each other, to disrupt the peace essential to liberty, and to subvert liberty itself. A second assumption is that however badly man may behave in a state of nature, he nevertheless is reasonable enough to understand that his condition can be improved. That understanding directs him to form a political society, for which he fortunately is qualified by a natural gregariousness and a capacity for government. A third assumption is that each man possesses certain natural rights, the most fundamental of which are the security of his life, his liberty, and his property. Being natural, the rights are therefore inviolable, and no institution nor person legitimately can alienate them.

Man's natural rights are the result of his natural behavior—its consequence or product. The philosophers of the Enlightenment assumed that each person sought to protect

first his *own* life, liberty, and possessions, that he was by
nature interested principally in his own welfare, that any
other course of behavior was unnatural and hence uncommon. If men were so inclined, that was because they either
were intended by the Deity to act in this way or were so
constituted psychologically as to make any other form of
behavior impossible. In either case, self-seeking had to be
taken as the datum of politics. To guarantee to each man
the right to seek his own interest became then the major
purpose of government. In the language of the Enlightenment, the purpose of government is the protection of natural rights. Stated in summary fashion, the protection of a
man's natural rights simply meant the protection of his
right to act naturally.

In a state of nature, these rights could not be secure,
because individuals would not respect the natural rights of
others. The problem of political organization was to find a
way of bringing men together which would enable each
person to seek his own interests without violating the interests of others. It perhaps needs underscoring that government did *not* have as its purpose the remaking of human
nature in order thereby to eliminate self-interest as the
cause of social discord. The classical liberals believed that
the state should take men as it finds them and they
would have been shocked (to say the least) by certain
later writers on government who in the name of freedom
wanted to refashion humanity in order to make it conform
to their notions of the good society.

The classic liberals solved the problem of political organization—the problem of bringing men together and of their
living usefully and peaceably—by means of the social contract. The social contract was an agreement between all
members of society about the conditions on which they
would combine and associate. As no man willingly would
agree to any form of government which deprived him of
his rights, and as the social contract could be concluded
only through voluntary agreement, the kind of government
so established would be necessarily one that represented
every individual and promoted his welfare. The social con-

tract occupied the central place in the political philosophy of the Enlightenment, because it represented the means whereby agreement was achieved and natural rights secured.

In the political remarks of the classical economists, the contract theory of government usually is rejected. Hume dismissed it as fanciful, and Smith believed it was unwarranted. Hume conceded that a contract once may have existed, but said that in the course of history it had become obliterated by violence and usurpation.[1] Smith argued against the idea in his *Lectures*, and in *The Wealth of Nations* declared that government initially was established to enforce an unequal distribution of wealth, remarking dryly that only under the wing of the civil magistrate could the rich get a good night's sleep.[2]

Yet even when the rejection of the social contract is given full weight, there will be found, I believe, an underlying consistency between the political philosophy of the Enlightenment and that of the classical economists. Behind the idea of an original contract, there was in classical liberalism a conception of human nature and a belief in natural rights. Though the economists rejected a literal interpretation of the contract and abandoned the idea of a providential force (the natural law) as the guiding force of men's social behavior, they did not depart significantly from the seventeenth century's view of human motives or from its ethical standards.

Hooker, Hobbes, and Locke, from whose work later liberal doctrine derives, may have meant to make a literal statement of the origins of government or they may have meant to describe the foundation on which government ought to rest. Whatever their intentions were, their writings were tracts for the times, and the times called for somewhat more freedom. The books performed their duty well, and we are richer today because of them. When Hume and Smith dismissed the assumption of an original contract, they were not disputing the idea that consent *ought* to form the basis of government but rather the belief that it actually *did*. Unfortunately they were not much more careful than the earlier philosophers in distinguishing between the actual and the ideal.

In his political essays, Hume observed that man by nature is factious, impulsive, ignorant of his best interests, and without sense enough to choose his own government. His intrinsic avarice, Hume declared, makes him covetous of the property of others and is the principal cause of social conflict (and also of progress).[3] Yet Hume found that these deficiencies were not fatal when he came to consider whether man's innate dignity was not more compelling than his meanness. Men are social creatures, he stated. Although they are not always rational (and not conspicuously rational ever) there is enough sense in the mass of them to make them capable eventually of self-government.[4] Their dignity manifests itself in two ways: in the power to conceive of perfection and in the ability to discern, respect, and to create "general opinion." The significance of this is made clear in the essay "Of the First Principles of Government." In the place of the social contract as the origin of government, Hume substituted "opinion." He said there are three "principles" (or beliefs) from which governments derive their authority: (a) individuals give allegiance to a government when they believe (i.e., are of the opinion) that it acts in their interest by providing certain general advantages, like the maintenance of law and order; (b) they believe a government that protects their property should be supported; (c) and they believe that a government of long standing has the right to rule simply because it is of long standing. In addition, there are secondary principles from which governments derive their authority. Individuals may support a government out of very narrowly regarded self-interest, in the expectation of a particular advantage, as distinct from the general advantage which comprises the first of the three principles noted above; or men may give their support to a government only because they are afraid to oppose it; or they may support it out of a personal devotion to the sovereign.[5]

Some of these principles (both "first" and "second") are rooted in human traits that Hume thought were dignified and others in traits that he thought were mean. One may infer that Hume in this essay was explaining the actual foundations of government and not the ideal. The most desirable government would base itself on the dignity in human nature, which is shown in the first two of the leading principles: the desire for peace and the desire for the protection of private property. These desires are in no way inconsistent with those established by Hooker, Locke, and Hobbes, nor are the conditions which, according to Hume, make the objectives realizable: the gregariousness of man and his ability to conceive of an ideal society. The explicit difference between Hume and his predecessors is over the social contract. But the difference is not decisive. Much more important is their agreement that government *should* be based on the consent of the governed. This idea was at the heart of the political doctrine of the Enlightenment. Although it does not appear in this form in Hume's essays, there does appear the idea of opinion, with the very strong suggestion that the ideal government draws its power from the opinion men hold of its ability to keep the peace and protect their property. And what is opinion, if it is not the idea of consent?

The classic liberals said that government ought to maintain peace and protect wealth. But that is not all it should do. When Locke wrote of the protection of property he clearly was interested in safeguarding more than the wealth of men. He meant "their lives, liberties and estates, which I call by the general name—property." [6] Property, so conceived, comprehended all natural rights. The duty of government is to protect and advance them. Hume did not say much about natural rights and he did not emphasize, as Locke and Hobbes did, the government's responsibility to protect them. But he certainly was not indifferent to freedom and security, which were the principal rights. The term "natural rights" appears rarely in classical economics except in *The Wealth of Nations* where, however, it usually applies to economic liberty. The political rights of the indi-

vidual frequently are described but are not stressed as
much as in the writings of the seventeenth century. The
want of emphasis suggests that political freedom was so
clearly and obviously a care of government that it did not
have to be asserted as forcibly as a century earlier when its
importance was not generally acknowledged. What called
for more emphasis in the eighteenth century was the fos-
tering of economic freedom. When one compares in the
works of Hobbes and Locke the small part occupied by the
doctrine of free exchange with the great emphasis given to
political freedom and security, one can understand why in
the works of Hume and Smith, writing in the next century,
economic freedom receives the greatest attention while political rights are taken almost as data. The former are famous for their exposition of the political rights of man and
are known hardly at all for their belief in a free market,
while the latter are noted almost wholly for advocating
free exchange and little at all for their political doctrine.
Yet there is no essential difference in either the economic or
the political doctrines of the two centuries.

UTILITY AND JUSTICE IN SMITH

The political doctrine of Smith does not depart from that
of Hume in any important way. It deserves separate men-
tion because of the emphasis utility receives and because
of Smith's specification of the just state. One may remark
that Smith's comments on government are permeated with
a cynicism which by comparison makes the tracts of his
skeptical friend, Hume, glow with sweetness and warmth.
In *The Wealth of Nations,* the motive of political behavior
(and most other) is self-interest, and self-interest operates
with indifferent success. His statements about government
here are fragmentary and must be taken with those in the
Lectures in order to secure a fairly complete conception of
his political doctrine. After a seemly acknowledgment of
the idea of sympathy (the basis, it will be recalled, of *The
Theory of Moral Sentiments*), Smith states in the *Lectures*
that governments are established in order to provide justice
and men learn that justice requires coercion—an idea

which, I think, is subsumed in Hume's principle of "general advantage." Governments are founded, therefore, on utility, which is their usefulness in providing justice. Justice consists of religious freedom, freedom of speech, the free use of property, and representative government. A government which deprives men of these liberties cannot be tolerated, and if resistance to it evokes violence, that is to be considered regrettable but hardly a reason for submission. Smith once observed that "rebels and heretics are those unlucky persons, who, when things have come to a certain degree of violence, have the misfortune to be of the weaker party." [7] Perhaps because he warmly cherished "the pretious right of private judgment, for the sake of which our forefathers kicked out the Pope and Pretender," and perhaps because he was less of the world than Hume, he could not become so agitated by the specter of revolution. [8] Both, however, were agreed that so long as a government demonstrated "any degree of moderation" (in taxation and its other powers) wisdom dictated it be supported. [9]

One must note all of the kinds of things that Smith expected of a just government. A reading of only *The Wealth of Nations* is apt to suggest that governments are founded solely to protect property. That men are avaricious, Smith certainly did say. He said also that they at times subordinate all other interests to their passion for property and he clearly implied that cupidity is at the root of most social disorder. But these traits do not exhaust the register of things that urge men to action nor do they comprehend all of those considerations, psychological and ethical, that Smith believed were relevant to political doctrine. As with Hume's politics, a distinction must be made between the actual and the ideal. Smith did say that governments came into existence in order to protect the wealthy from the poor. But he did not say that this was reason enough to support them. A government had to do much more. The kind he most desired was one that would protect those "pretious" rights for which his ancestors fought and which were declaimed so movingly by Locke, Hobbes, and Hooker. Although he did not believe (as they may have) that the English state was founded originally on a social contract, he did believe, when he stated that men seek justice through political association, that consent should form the basis of government.

A literal interpretation of the social contract was the only important issue that separated the political doctrine of the classical economists from that of the Enlightenment. The psychological and ethical assumptions of the two were the same. Indeed, the seventeenth century taught the eighteenth the elements of liberal political philosophy, namely, that men are avaricious, that they are mean and belligerent but that their rational faculty and gregarious instinct are strong enough to bring them together under a government that will protect their lives, liberties, and estates.

2 The Paradox of Economic and Political Freedom

The classical economists were not prepared to carry their political liberalism to its implied conclusion, namely, universal enfranchisement and popular control of all branches of the government. On the other hand, the economists did not expressly place any limits on freedom when they said that a free market was the ideal method of organizing the economy. Instead, they implied or stated that economic freedom was a natural right. Does this opposition of economic and political doctrine—of believing in complete economic freedom but limited political freedom—denote a contradiction in their liberalism? A common view is that the classical economists were spokesmen for the emergent capitalism of their time and were devoted only to the liberty of their special charge, the middle class. In this view their conception of economic freedom was in fact as limited as their conception of political freedom. I do not accept this view. I believe there really was a paradox in their economic and political ideas.

THE ECONOMISTS AND THE MIDDLE CLASS

The classicists believed in economic freedom for everyone and not just for the middle class. They argued most persuasively for the freedom of the latter, but there is no evidence that it was their exclusive concern. Their sympathy for the lower classes was demonstrated in many ways. Hume declared that an equal distribution of income was most consistent with human nature, that it best promoted the national welfare, and was most conducive to the extension of liberty, even though under certain conditions it might create conflict.[10] Smith gave the workingman the most important function in the economy, upbraided employers for combining to drive down wages, heaped scorn on the manners and morals of businessmen, and in so many ways evinced his hostility to the middle class, even though he defended its right to trade freely, that he hardly can be called its champion.[11] The desire of Malthus to see the poor and propertyless sheltered from as much distress as possible led him to be skeptical of a policy of laisser faire. Ricardo in many ways disclosed his humanitarian feelings, despite his reputation as an impersonal and remorseless logician. He made his productivity ethics the justification for raising wages; he was opposed to any sudden repeal of the laws providing relief to the poor, favoring instead their gradual elimination in order to prevent "overwhelming distress." [12] He was receptive to measures that might improve the condition of the poor, advocating in his *Principles* that the legislature make some effort to discourage large families and that society at large persuade the lower classes that prudence and forethought were both necessary and "profitable" virtues.[13] In 1819, he agreed to serve as a member of a committee to examine the proposal of Robert Owen, the utopian socialist. Although he disagreed with Owen on most points he gave the proposal a thorough and fair hearing.[14] That the object of the classicists was the welfare of all society, and not that of the middle class only, was stated most explicitly by M'Culloch. He said of the work of the political economist:

He is not to frame systems, and devise schemes, for increasing the wealth and enjoyments of particular classes; but to apply himself to discover the sources of national wealth and universal prosperity, and the means by which they may be rendered most productive.[15]

When, however, the economists considered the proper extent of political freedom, their views were not as comprehensive. They did not believe the people in their entirety should have as much opportunity to make political decisions as to make economic decisions. That *some* liberty should be allowed to everyone they did believe—but that all should have the same liberty they did *not* believe.

Not all of the classical economists wrote about the structure of government and the extent of the suffrage. Those who did proposed various limitations on the suffrage and on the number of public officials who should be chosen by election. Hume favored a hereditary monarch. He was opposed to the election of the chief officer of government and was opposed also to any tampering with the right of succession. This is made quite plain in his essay "On the Protestant Succession." After considering the legitimacy of the claims of the Stuarts and of the Hanovers who displaced them, Hume acknowledged that by reason of antiquity and heredity the Stuarts clearly belonged on the throne and the Hanovers did not. But, he continued, the Hanovers happened to be there and the Stuarts were in exile. To try to depose the Hanovers would be so disruptive that no man in his right mind would suggest it. Such reasoning seems guided by the maxim, Whatever is, is right, and to make Hume's politics follow the rule of *laisser être* as his economics followed *laisser faire*. That impression, however, is erroneous, because Hume in his political works gave greatest emphasis to the need for authority, to peace and order, as the conditions of liberty—as opposed to legitimacy or obedience—and he valued a government in the measure to which it met these needs. What Hume did in this essay was in fact to reduce the conventional doctrine of monarchy to an absurdity. He stated that it did not matter who was king as long as he performed his function tolerably well, that the king ruled not by divine right or by the authority of succession but simply to provide the stability which government needed. One may imagine how the Jacobites and the partisans of the Hanovers reacted to this tract. One feels one knows how Hume reacted to them—no doubt in the same way that he viewed the hairsplitting of the Molenists and Jansenists, with their "thousand unintelligible disputes, which are not worthy the reflection of a man of sense."

Smith too was opposed to a government in which all officers were elected. In his *Lectures,* he listed three forms of government: "monarchical," in which power is vested in one person "who can do what he pleases"; "aristocratical," in which power is held by a small group that achieves status because of family or wealth; and "democratical," in which the "management of affairs belongs to the whole body of the people together." The second and the third were, he said, "republican," the term being used to denote a government without an hereditary, single magistrate.[16] Smith did not wholly approve of any of the three, but favored a form of the third combined with a monarch, holding that a king was necessary for preserving order among contending economic interests and political factions.[17]

THE FRANCHISE

Neither Hume nor Smith wrote specifically about the extent of the franchise. They probably approved of the property qualification which was commonly attached to the vote in the eighteenth century (and later). The limitation is consistent with their doctrine and they nowhere opposed it, expressly or by implication. Among the economists James Mill was the first who explicitly formulated the details of a proper franchise. In his extraordinary *Essay on Government* (so deductive that it made Macaulay think of the propositions of geometry), Mill stated that the privilege of voting should be restricted to those persons whose private interests were identical with the interests of the community. He deduced that they came mainly from the middle and working classes, who fortunately comprise the majority of the community. Not everyone in the majority is, however, capable of making political decisions and hence of voting. The right to vote was to be limited to those of proven ability. Mill tried to prove that political ability is revealed in certain outward signs, principally of age and the possession of property, and he made them the conditions of the suffrage. The age qualification is placed quite high but the property qualification is made very low in order to include in the electorate more than are excluded from it. He dismissed the inclusion of women in the suffrage. His language was curt and contemptuous. So too was the language used fifty years later by John Stuart Mill to ridicule those who would *exclude* them.[18]

The universal franchise was viewed skeptically, though briefly, by Senior in his *Outline of the Science of Political Economy*. He later wrote of it at length in his review of Lord Brougham's *Political Philosophy* and elaborated a point he made earlier that not only is politics "the most difficult of all sciences" but its difficulty is scarcely recognized, with the consequence that ability is most scarce where it is most needed. Until the mass of the people give more evidence of understanding the point, popular government—in which the suffrage is universal and all offices elective—was not feasible, he said.[19] To support his point Senior adduced the behavior of the American people of the generation preceding the Civil War.

M'Culloch in writing of the relation between economic and political liberty did not see any great necessity for individuals to have political freedom along with economic freedom, although he acknowledged that free governments were more likely than absolute governments to promote economic progress.[20]

3 Human Nature, History, and Government

In the foregoing description of the economists' ideas of economic and political freedom there is a clear paradox. Its source is in the utilitarian basis of their politics. To understand the source one must recall the circumstances of the last half of the eighteenth and of the early nineteenth centuries and relate them to what the economists said about the structure of government. Their ideas about representation seem to have been formed by two considerations. One was a distrust of the ability of the people for self-government, and the other an opposition to strong government. The economists' statements on the extent of political liberty suggest they sought to avoid both a condition in which the people possessed full power and one in which power was concentrated in a small group. Of the two, it was probably the latter they most feared. This interpretation is based on the frequent assertions in the works of the economists (and of others of the same period) that a government founded upon a universal franchise is necessarily unstable and disorderly, that it must terminate in a despotism exercised by a small minority at the expense of all other groups in the community, including the originally enfranchised majority. (Many eighteenth-century writers distinguished between an *absolute* government, which was one based on law and administered by a minority and an *arbitrary* government which was one in which the minority recognized no law and acknowledged no limit to its power. The economists, however, were not among the writers who made this distinction, because they believed that any ruling minority would necessarily become willful, arbitrary, and dictatorial. Therefore I have used the words "absolute," "arbitrary," and "authoritarian" synonymously.)

THE CONCEPTION OF HUMAN NATURE

The distrust of popular government appears to have come partly from the economists' conception of human nature and partly from historical circumstances. In the political philosophy of the Enlightenment and of the classical economists one of the leading ideas was (as noted above) that property is the major cause of social disorder. Men are naturally covetous and restrain themselves only for reasons of a larger self-interest and never out of benevolence or justice. Hence there are only two means open to a government for maintaining social peace. It either must suppress all acquisitive behavior, thereby removing the cause of disorder, or it must devise a way to make the self-interest of each individual consistent with that of all others in order that the liberty of all of them be increased.

The first alternative was rejected by the liberals—in the seventeenth century because it was a violation of man's natural right to increase his wealth as long as he injured no one else, and in the eighteenth because suppression was futile as well as wrong. The other alternative—that of reconciling the self-interest of individuals—was the basis of representative government in those two centuries. In order that the behavior of each person would promote the welfare of others as well as of himself, political representation (the economists believed) should be given to those who had a private interest in keeping the peace and withheld from those who did not. Those with property had an interest in supporting government, as a law-enforcing agency, and so they were included in the suffrage; but the propertyless did not have this interest and hence were excluded. This limitation was not imposed because the economists believed the poor were covetous and other people were not. Everyone was thought to be covetous. But men of property could be more depended upon to restrain themselves: first, because having a private interest to be protected they were more aware of the general interest served by government; and second, because they wished to protect this private interest even though by so doing they sacrificed the possibility of a larger gain (the implication being that they favored a certain smaller sum to an uncertain larger one). The propertyless, however, had nothing to lose. They conceivably would gamble on a political upheaval on the chance of acquiring some fortune. In a less extreme case they might seek to improve their position by legislation that discriminated against wealth (which, in the economists' view, invariably reacted to the disadvantage of the poor as well as of the rich). In summary, the psychology of the classical economists dictated the exclusion of the poor from the franchise, because their covetousness would bring social disorder if permitted to express itself politically.

Why should the poor be given *any* opportunity to express themselves, politically or otherwise, if their natural inclinations lead them to disorder and violence? If men will abuse their political liberty, they will, *a fortiori*, abuse their economic liberty. This difficulty can be removed by recalling (from the preceding chapter) that the classical economists did not think *much* damage could come from individual economic activity, *as long as it remained individual,* that is, as long as it was competitive. Each individual in seeking to increase his wealth was restrained from doing serious injury to others by law and custom and more compellingly by the competitive activity of others. The economic damage from unrestrained acquisitiveness took the form of a reduction in the aggregate quantity of goods and services and of a redistribution of income—both of which would be disclosed in changes in prices. In a competitive economy no individual could have any effect on the prices of the things he bought or sold. However much he may have wished to influence prices, he was prevented from doing so by the competing activity of others. This I take to be the meaning of Smith's statement that once competition is established, although it cannot prevent individuals from *wishing* to do injury to others, it will prevent "the mean rapacity, the monopolizing spirit of merchants and manufacturers . . . from disturbing the tranquillity of anybody but themselves." [21]

Political activity by its nature cannot be competitive— so one infers. If the members of a class have common interests, if it was given full freedom of action, and if it was the most numerous, there would be nothing to prevent it from imposing its will on everyone else. To give such a class complete political liberty would surely result, the economists reasoned, in the destruction of the liberty of everyone. The poor were regarded as just such a class. As the economists believed that economic freedom should be denied to all who would use it to injure others (monopolists, for example), so they also believed that political freedom

should not be given to those who would destroy the freedom of others.

THE RECORD OF BEHAVIOR

The economists' conception of human behavior was supported by the social conditions of their age and by the les-
sons which they saw in history. Nearly all of the classical
school were historically minded, and none more so than
Hume. He was also the most skeptical of popular government. The history of the efforts at self-government seemed
to them to be a record of failure on which there was en-
grossed a warning against giving the people power enough
to choose their own rulers.

When they turned from history to their own society,
they saw some improvement in the condition of the
people but not enough to disallow the lesson of the past.
Many lived in distress, and the great majority still were
preoccupied with the mechanics of existence. The mass of
men had little time, energy, or interest for the cultivating
of political talents. Crime was frequent and brutal. The enforcement of the law was lax and at times negligible; usually it was left to night watchmen who often were crim-
inals themselves. On the country roads, robbery and assault
were common and a part of the expected hazards of travel.
Once the roads did become safe, Britons were several generations in becoming accustomed to safety as a normal
condition. "Can you not walk from one end of England to
another in perfect security? I ask you whether, the world
over or in past history, there is anything like that? Nothing." So spoke one of the early figures of the Manchester
School of economics, J. A. Roebuck, a Philosophic Radical
and friend of John Mill. Matthew Arnold quoted this to
illustrate his description of a Philistine[22]—the same Arnold,
the reader will recall, who found Marcus Aurelius so completely admirable. And yet Roebuck was one of the end
products of what the Stoics began, however outrageous
the connection will seem to those of Arnold's view. Freedom *does* require personal safety.

Drunkenness was common and a major problem. It was

a problem to the military, which could not find enough physically fit recruits; to the parish authorities, because of extensive indigence and neglect of families; and to the state, because of the high mortality rate from diseases having their origin in alcoholism. When for a time the common people left off these habits and interested themselves in politics, they turned, in the most celebrated liberal cause of the eighteenth century, to the support of John Wilkes who had been deprived unlawfully of his seat in Parliament. Wilkes, as it happened, was not meant for the role of people's champion; in fact, his defense of representative government was almost inadvertent. If he had been a different sort of person and if there had been more order in his private affairs, this phase of the political education of the people would have presented its issues more clearly and its achievement (for Wilkes was reseated) more lastingly. In all, the condition of the common people, their manners and morals, offered little to suggest a capacity for self-government.

What they knew of psychology, history, and from observation led the economists to oppose popular government and led them to oppose also those forms of government that concentrated power in a small group or in one person. As stated above, their ideas of representation were conditioned by the fear of centralized authority as well as by a distrust of self-government. They believed both extremes must be avoided if the liberty of the individual was to be advanced. A centralized government exercising large powers, such as an absolute monarchy or an oligarchy, presented a danger that although exactly the opposite was just as real as the danger of a state based on universal enfranchisement. A popularly elected government could not serve freedom because it could not establish the prior condition of social peace. An authoritarian government never would advance beyond the establishment of peace to the granting of freedom to its subjects.

In their view of human nature, the economists (as stated before) gave a large place to self-interest and believed it usually was stronger than any altruism or benevolence the individual might feel. This view made them as skeptical of an authoritarian government as of a popular one. That every man will, if he can, subject others to himself was a belief which they put among the first of their first principles of politics. This belief was expressed in many ways: by Hume when he declared that man's sense of justice was feeble before the sense of his own interest; by Smith when he declared that the violence and injustice of the rulers of mankind were an ancient evil dictated by "the nature of human affairs"; and most plainly by James Mill when he said:

> That one human being will desire to render the person and property of another subservient to his pleasures, not withstanding the pain or loss of pleasure it may occasion to that other individual, is the foundation of Government.[23]

Even John Stuart Mill, who lived at a more amiable time, said a natural disposition of mankind was to wish to tyrannize over one another.[24] Against this background, Lord Acton's famous remark about power is an epigrammatic summary of the wisdom of two centuries. (Like most epigrams it is an annoying, even mischievous, half-truth, the other half of which is, according to Allen N. Herzog, that an inadequate amount of power is corrupting and no power at all is absolutely corrupting.)

It was not only their psychology that led the classical economists to oppose authoritarian government. Historical observation and the experience of government in their own age also influenced them. Still fresh in meaning, although they had happened a century before, were the English revolutions that overthrew the despotism of the Stuarts and of the Puritans and established the supremacy of constitutional government. Even nearer in time and significance were the political conditions on the Continent. Such facts could only strengthen the view that liberty was impossible in an absolute state. The view was so consistent with the tradition of classical liberalism, with which the eighteenth century began, that it hardly needs explaining. One may note, however, that there was a great difference between the British classicists and the French physiocrats over the issue of absolute government. The physiocrats, while believing that each man should have the liberty to pursue his economic interests in his own way, were also defenders of absolute monarchy. When *The Wealth of Nations* was published, the physiocrats found much in it of interest, but certainly nothing could have seemed more curious than the author's strictures on statesmen, rulers, and politicians, from whom he expected nothing enlightened either in the form of despotic rule or any other kind.

4 The Nationalism of the Economists

The aversion of the economists toward concentrated power —which made them oppose absolute government—also made them advocate a strong national state. When their nationalism is set against their belief in free trade, there emerges a second paradox. Actually, the paradox is double-edged. There seems to be as much inconsistency in believing a government should have only limited power over its subjects and great power to confront other states as there is in believing in both free trade and national power.

The purely political side of the paradox—the opposition between believing the government should have limited power at home and great power abroad—I can explain only by saying that British liberalism *was* nationalistic. Its principles emerged from the history of the people who made up Great Britain; they were meant to describe that people's social policy and to direct them. One would be pleased to believe that the liberals had as generous a view of foreigners as of their countrymen, that they brought the entire world within the compass of their ideas, and that their object was the welfare of the nations. But they did not think this way at all. They did not even include western Europe in their view. When Hume declared he wanted the French and Germans to prosper, he said he did so as an Englishman.[25] I do not think the economists had any animosity toward foreigners, and they certainly kept themselves apart from the crude parochialism of the time. But they were not prepared to sacrifice the wealth and liberty of the British to the people of other countries.

THE EXCEPTIONS TO FREE TRADE

The economic aspect of the paradox is more important than the political. The paradox itself emerges (as stated above) from the fact that if free trade was carried as far as it profitably can be carried, national states would be impossible or unlikely. There is considerable evidence that the economists did not wish to carry free trade this far. Hume was against free trade if it reduced the military power of the nation. Moreover, in a significant passage he favored a protective tariff not only to hasten the development of industries that eventually would become efficient but also to encourage those that otherwise never would exist.[26]

The exceptions to free trade are even more pronounced in *The Wealth of Nations*. Smith defended the Navigation Acts as the wisest of all restrictive legislation, because "defense . . . is of much more importance than opulence." When he passed from the general principle that should govern international trade to specific measures of trade policy, he advocated a surprising amount of restriction. He said a tariff was permissible (*a*) if it promoted national defense, (*b*) if it enabled one nation to force others into free trade, (*c*) if by the repeal of a specific duty legitimate vested interests would suffer, and (*d*) if a domestic product competing with an import was taxed. Finally, he said, there could be "a sort of reasons of state" which justify suspending free trade.[27]

(The distinctive feature of Smith's mind is disclosed in passages like these, which qualify a general proposition and relate it to particular problems, as here he qualifies the idea that free trade is the most efficient way to organize the international market. At constructing general propositions, Smith was less gifted than the best of his contemporaries. He was much less original than Hume. He also was verbose where Hume was brief and was unclear where Hume was lucid. In putting propositions together into a general system which was complete, coherent, and logical,

Smith was even worse. He does not compare with Ricardo at that sort of thing, which today is called model building. Most intellectual historians agree that Smith was not particularly original and that he certainly was not logical. They would say, however, that he was a great empiricist and that his marshaling of the facts was what made his conceptual structure distinguished. I would disagree even with this. He certainly was empirically minded, but often he was wrong about the facts. For example, many of the trade restrictions which he deplored were actually no longer in effect when he wrote. At times he not only was pushing at an open door but besieging institutions which already had surrendered. What seems to me to have been his great achievement was to move from general propositions to their particular application, to separate what was relevant and useful in them from what was not, to qualify, amend, and adapt ideas so that they would be helpful in solving specific problems. At this kind of work he had no equal. It is a work calling for a mind that is inquiring without being merely curious, skeptical but not pessimistic, tough but not unchangeable, and above all common-sensible and yet not prosaic. His good sense was his great glory.)

The work of Ricardo also reveals national feelings, despite the rigor with which he upheld the benefits of free exchange. In discussing the reasons why resources do not move freely across national boundaries, he stated that non-economic considerations were paramount. The emigration of capital is hampered, he said, by the "natural disinclination" which every man feels to quit the country of his birth and connections. He added that these are "feelings which I should be sorry to see weakened." [28]

INDIVIDUAL FREEDOM AND NATIONAL POWER

Such national feelings expressed a more fundamental belief of the economists. It was that each nation must have power enough to secure its sovereignty. This belief in turn comes from their ideas of order and liberty. The paradox between nationalism and free trade can be resolved by examining Hume's conception of the relation between liberty and national power. The state, he said, must have enough power to prevent liberty from falling into license, and the people must be powerful enough to protect themselves against the state. But that is not all. There is also a danger to liberty and order from those states that do not have a free constitution. That danger alone would have led the economists to support national power.

Conceivably the liberties of the people could be protected by the amalgamation of independent nations into one grand political unit, but this was impossible within the precepts of the economists', and particularly of Hume's, political doctrine. A world government could maintain itself only by an amount of power that was inconsistent with freedom. Such a government would have within its authority all of those powers by which, Hume believed, tyranny came to be established. Because its territories would be separated and widely distant, there could be no adequate communication among citizens. The dispersion of territories would enable the government to subvert the liberty of outlying areas and then move inward until all liberty had been destroyed. The chief officer of such a government necessarily would be remote from the people, which would engender a superstitious reverence for him. Hume believed that liberty and order are served best in small states, where the citizens can communicate easily with each other, where each region is aware of what is happening in others, and where the sovereign is always before the eyes of the people, who, seeing him in the regular business of government, come to realize that he is an ordinary mortal as fallible as they and no more worthy of reverence. Moreover, should something occur to disrupt social peace, a small state imposes limits to the spread of popular delusion; conversely, its relatively small area places limits on the extension of tyranny if once that should be attempted.[29]

The paradox of free trade and nationalism is to be explained, then, as a manifestation of the economists' hostility to absolute government. They believed in free trade as the principle which should guide the economic relations among states, but they also believed in qualifying the principle in order to avoid its interfering with national power. An unqualified application of free trade (including the free movement of labor) is possible only in a world state. To the economists, however, the governing of any but a relatively small area required an exercise of power which they thought incompatible with the protection of liberty. They were forced to compromise either their belief in economic liberty or in political liberty, and it was the former that was modified.

5 *The Structure of Government*

The economists favored a particular form, or structure, of government, and it was derived from their ideas about political behavior and about the purpose of government. They favored a form in which power would be distributed among two or three groups in such a way that each person would have some freedom but not enough to deprive other persons of their freedom. I say "some" rather than complete freedom, because every person would not have all of the powers that have come to comprise the characteristics of a free government. Every person would be assured of government by law, but not all of them would have the power, through the vote or other means, of participating in the making of law.

POLITICAL EQUILIBRIUM

This structure of government was described in different words by the economists who wrote about it. Whatever it was called, its features were the same in the writing of Hume, Smith, James Mill, and Senior. It appears by implication in some of the Parliamentary speeches by Ricardo. The conception was simple and clear. It held that society consisted of the governed and the governors. The mass of the people comprised most, but not all, of the first group. That group was to express itself in the lower house of Parliament, to the extent that it was to express itself at all. Parliament could not be allowed to rule alone. It had to be restrained, and the restraint would be exercised by what frequently was described as the "aristocratical interest," that interest would express itself in an upper house, the Lords, or through a royal family, or both. The purpose of the House of Lords and of the monarchy was to prevent a representative government from abusing its power. The Lords and monarchy, that is, would contribute order and stability while the Commons would provide freedom. The belief in limited representation was not a justification of aristocracy and monarchy. That rationalization runs in quite a different direction and follows from an assumption that there is a class which by reason of its superior talents and exclusive political wisdom necessarily should be given power. The economists, in their conception of human nature, ascribed the same motives to the upper classes as to the lower and believed neither was to be trusted with a monopoly of power. Their object was a government that would establish an equilibrium among competing interest groups. That would be done by distributing power in such a way that no group would become paramount but each would have power enough to express its permissible interests. The theory of such a government is the familiar one of checks and balances. It was one of the ideas for which the eighteenth century is famous. It is found in many of the political papers of the period, and was set forth most impressively in *The Federalist* (as Chapter 3, Vol. 1 of this book explains).

Most of the economists did not write systematic political works and did not develop the idea fully. But they did present its essential features. Hume declared that liberty most probably would succeed in a society in which the government was strong enough to maintain order and did not have to fear popular resistance, and in which the people were strong enough to exercise their rights and need not fear the government. Such a society would be governed by "checks and controls, provided by the constitution." [30] Of the views of Smith, there is no better summary than what the Earl of Buchan said of them:

He approached to republicanism in his political principles, and considered a commonwealth as the platform for the monarchy, hereditary succession in the chief magistrate being necessary only to prevent the commonwealth from being shaken by ambition or absolute dominion introduced by the consequences of contending factions.[31]

Although James Mill denied the possibility of an exact "balance of power" among the democratic, aristocratic, and royal interests in society, he nevertheless proposed a governmental structure consisting of "checking bodies." The legislative branch, to be chosen by an extensive although not a universal suffrage, would restrain the aristocracy and monarchy, and would advance the democratic interest. The aristocracy would be represented by a body serving as a check on the legislature. An hereditary monarch would discharge the administrative and judicial functions of government.[32]

Senior favored a "mixed" form of government, in which the people would have representation enough to protect liberty and the aristocracy and monarchy enough power to secure order.[33] Ricardo's views on the structure of government are suggested in a speech he made on the suffrage. There is in the speech a strong implication that he looked with approval on the House of Lords. Since he usually was in the radical wing of Commons, one may assume that his approval was not given out of sympathy for an aristocratic form of government. One may infer that his position on this point was similar to that of the other classical economists and that he favored the continuation of the House of Lords (which, he stated, the people also wanted preserved) because it provided a necessary restraining element in government.[34]

6 Economic Improvement and Social Progress

Out of the nationalistic feelings of the classical economists and their conception of the structure of government, there emerges the idea of a strong national state based on law.

In it power is limited enough to leave each man free in the pursuit of his legitimate interests and great enough to protect him from the encroachments of others in his own country and from abroad. Sovereignty in such a state rests ultimately with the electorate, and the electorate is to consist only of persons possessing some property. The limitation was necessary, the economists said, because men without property could not be expected to exercise the franchise in the interest of order and liberty. This belief in turn was derived from their conception of human nature; it was strengthened by their interpretation of past efforts of self-government, and by the condition of the lower classes in their age.

The limitation on freedom was not, however, something to be imposed forever. If the circumstances which made it necessary were to change, the amount of freedom which the people properly could exercise would change also. The major prerequisite for more freedom was an increase in the real income of the masses. Their poverty was the main cause of whatever social disorder and tyranny that existed, and the reduction of poverty would, the economists believed, make society more orderly, stable, and free. They have a great reputation for being pessimists; actually the classical economists believed society could be greatly improved. If they had believed anything else, their beliefs would have been anomalous indeed, since progress was a byword of their age.

THE CONDITION OF PROGRESS

The issue to which they directed their attention was not the possibility of progress—that was taken for granted—but the circumstances most favorable to it. They believed that in the free market they had found what was most favorable. If men had the liberty of trading freely and if their property was secure, economic progress would follow "naturally," meaning not providentially but as a matter of course. The accumulation of capital would raise the real income of the masses, and two important changes would occur. They would acquire an interest in supporting the existing order, an order of the kind the economists regarded as ideal. And they would be able to attend to their moral and mental improvement. Then, by reason both of desire and ability, the masses would deserve complete political liberty. I want to emphasize their belief that the condition of political progress was an increase in real income and that the condition of such an increase was an extension of economic freedom (but not complete laisser faire by any means). This belief was a part of a larger conception of the classical economists that the improvement of morals and manners, and progress in the arts and sciences, could advance only as men were free to seek their material welfare in their own way. In this conception the political and economic doctrines of the classicists are most closely related.

The relationship was made clear in many ways. Hume saw in the development of a free market the raising of the moral level of society. He said that as "commerce" diffused its benefits throughout all ranks of society, the coarse and baleful aspects of acquisitiveness would disappear and honor and virtue would replace them.[35] Throughout his essays there is disclosed the belief that as liberty becomes more extensive, the material and political welfare of the people is raised and their intellectual and moral qualities as well. Even though he was distrustful of self-government in his own time, he saw the likelihood of its eventual establishment. He stated:

It has also been found, as the experience of mankind increases, that the *people* are no such dangerous monsters as they have been represented, and that it is in every respect better to guide them like rational creatures than to lead or drive them like brute beasts.[36]

Smith, more than any of the economists, wrote about the relation between economic activity and social progress. He made the development of a free society depend on the extension of economic freedom; and he made the development of virtue and wisdom, on which, he believed, self-government must rely, depend on raising the material welfare of the people.[37] Although Ricardo did not express himself directly on this point, he probably agreed with Smith, believing as he did that "the general happiness" of mankind was increased as its income increased, and that the method of increasing income was a free market.[38]

The dependence of cultural development upon material welfare was expressed most completely by M'Culloch who said:

Where wealth has not been amassed, individuals, being constantly occupied in providing for their immediate wants, have no time left for the culture of their minds; so that their views, sentiments, and feelings, become alike contracted and illiberal. The possession of a decent competence, or the power to indulge in other pursuits than those which directly tend to satisfy our animal wants and desires, is necessary to soften the selfish passions; to improve the moral and intellectual character; and to ensure any considerable proficiency in liberal studies and pursuits. And hence, the acquisition of wealth is not desirable merely as the means of procuring immediate and direct gratifications, but is indispensably necessary to the advancement of society in civilization and refinement.[39]

What the economists believed about progress made their view of representative government considerably more liberal than it otherwise would have been. The amount of order which a state must impose as a practical necessity, and the extent of liberty which of moral necessity it must cultivate, both depend on the material condition of the majority of the people. The better is that condition, the more capable are the people of governing themselves, the more liberty are they able to exercise, and the less is the amount of coercion the state need use. The economists believed that the material condition of society would improve, and hence they also were confident that its government would become more free—that the masses would achieve political liberty commensurate with their economic liberty.

A NOTE ON MILL

In the nineteenth century such an improvement in the real income of the people did occur. When John Stuart Mill, the last of the classical school, wrote of government, he allowed a far greater amount of liberty and insisted on much less order than his predecessors had. I have refrained from considering his political ideas here, except incidentally, because they belong to a period much different from that in which the earlier economists wrote. (His economic policy is described in the next chapter.) His view of the function of government was much more extensive than that of the earlier economists, not only because he lived in a more complex society but also (and more fundamentally) because his ideas were more utilitarian than theirs and more influenced by Helvetius, Holbach, and Bentham than by Hooker, Locke, and Hume. He was not as averse as his predecessors in the classical school to regarding individuals as instruments to be improved and manipulated in the hands of a wise and beneficent government. Yet he did, in many other ways, exemplify the tradition of the earlier economists. His conception of the ideal government was as relative as theirs, and he said even more explicitly than they that the best government for a society is that which is best adapted to the capacities of its members. These capacities were far larger in his age than they were half a century or more earlier. So far had the people of the Western world, and especially those of Great Britain, revealed their worth that Mill urged an extensive though not entirely universal franchise as most consistent with the quality of his age.

In the nineteenth century there not only was a growing belief that the government could do with fewer coercive political powers because the people were better able to exercise their freedom with restraint. There also was a belief among some that the power of the government in international affairs properly should be diminished. As the belief of the economists in self-government increased, so too did their nationalistic feeling diminish. Certain of them, and the political leaders who shared their principles, strongly believed in restraining the foreign policy of Great Britain, in maintaining an indifferent attitude to the troubles of the Continent, and in vigorously opposing the expansion of the empire. Better, they said, that the energies of Britain be directed toward increasing its trade than to meddling in other people's affairs.

That was the view of Cobden and Bright and the Manchester school, which more than any other was responsible for putting the idea of free trade into practice. It also agitated for world peace and for extending the franchise. The Manchester school carried the classical ideas of political liberty and economic liberty in foreign trade (but *only* foreign trade) to their ultimate conclusion. The ideas were applied so ruthlessly that the economists of the period (and most were in the classical tradition) stood apart from the school. That, however, is another event, and I have described it elsewhere.[40]

LIBERALISM
IN THE GREAT CENTURY

The nineteenth century usually is thought to have been the greatest age of economic liberalism, greater than any other, from its origins in Stoicism down to the present time. Economists think of the century as the long afternoon of the ideology. They believe it then meant laisser faire and that laisser faire was the policy of Great Britain, the major economy of the world. In fact, the century was not like that, and historians have tried to tell us so. They have reported the many ways in which the British government intervened in the market. The historians also have said the intervention was inconsistent with liberalism. In this they are, in my opinion, mistaken. The intervention can most of it be explained as an application of the doctrine—not, to be sure, an application of the liberalism of free markets, anarchy, the constable, and the other elements that erroneously and often are taken to be its exclusive meaning. The intervention was an application of what the doctrine had come to be by the nineteenth century. The purpose of this chapter is to explain what that was.

1 The Importance of the Nineteenth Century

The century was important for a number of reasons: (1) The intellectual authority of economic liberalism was greater than at any other time. (2) Nevertheless its principles were not well understood, were not even clear, and were a matter for dispute among the liberals themselves as well as for their opponents. (3) Its political authority was

however immense. (4) The first effort to make a comprehensive statement of its principles was in 1848. (5) There
was substantial opposition to economic liberalism throughout the century. (6) The doctrine and its practice had to
contend with difficult economic problems.

1. The ideas of economic liberalism, which had been
gathering force for centuries, came to their full power in
the nineteenth century. They informed the statements
about policy made by the orthodox (classical) economists and they were the power with which dissent from
orthodoxy had to reckon. No one could write or speak
about policy without acknowledging the power. How
it influenced the writings of the economists is explained
in this chapter. But its influence went much beyond them
and extended to the social philosophers, the literary people,
the opponents of classical economics, the journalists, pamphleteers, politicians, mass leaders, agitators, and others.
Liberalism had many different meanings to these people.
But one generalization can be made. To almost all who
believed in it and to some who did not, liberalism did not
mean laisser faire—that is, it did not mean a policy of nonintervention by the government and of allowing the major
economic decisions to be made on unregulated markets.
The rejection of laisser faire was one of the few ideas on
which there was nearly complete agreement among the
economists and between them and the political leaders.

2. About other ideas there was much less agreement.
They were moreover unclear and incomplete, especially in
the first half of the century. While there was agreement
that a state had the right, in liberal doctrine, to intervene
in the economy, there was no agreement about what the
purposes of intervention should be, about how much was
permissible, and what methods could be used. The reason for the disagreement was the unsettled condition of
the ideas of policy. Although the classical economists are
reputed to have been champions of the free market, they
really did not have ideas about policy that were comprehensive enough to make them champions of anything, at
least until 1848 (and it may be argued not even then).

It is not often noticed that the first comprehensive statement of classical economic policy—or the first effort to make a statement—came only in 1848, almost a century after Hume brought classicism into being (and more than a century if one dates its origin earlier). Smith, Bentham, James Mill, Ricardo, M'Culloch, Senior, and Torrens are the great in the register of the classical school, which, in the popular view, was directed by a faith in laisser faire. But none in fact declared himself for it. What is more interesting is that none of them wrote about policy in a systematic way—that is, in a way that would make clear to their readers just what liberalism stood for, that would be helpful to the public in appraising measures of policy and to legislators in enacting them, or that would enable their followers to bring together their discursive remarks into a synthetic statement. John Stuart Mill was the first to do this—to enunciate a *theory* of policy—and he did it in his *Principles*, which was published in 1848. That was two years after Great Britain had taken one of the last steps toward free foreign trade, by repealing the Corn Laws. Mill was not enthusiastic about their repeal, although he was strongly in favor of the very last step, the repeal of the Navigation Acts in 1854.

3. Even though their ideas of policy were not complete or clear, the economists had great influence on the political figures of the period and through them on the public at large. Burke had said of his time that it was the age of the economists, but the nineteenth century was more truly so, from Waterloo to the last government of Gladstone in 1894. There never was a time when the public was on more familiar terms with economics, when opinion was as much under its influence, and when governments were more respectful of its "laws." Economists were listened to for their political economy—for the purposes of their policy and not only its means. They were not expert advisers or skilled technicians; they were political men. Thomas Tooke was known as the schoolmaster of the House of Commons, and a schoolmaster in the nineteenth century was a man of parts. A prime minister called John Mill the Saint of Ra-

tionalism. There were economists in Parliament and cabinets, and economists were called on by Select Committees for their opinion on political goals as well as on the economic means for attaining them. Whether called on or not, they usually expressed their opinions. Also noteworthy is the fact that the leading economists took part in the greatest political movement of the century—the reform of Parliament and the extension of the franchise. The literate world today unfortunately knows little about the political causes with which the economists were associated. They denounced the restriction of civil liberties following the Napoleonic Wars, demanded the right of all to freedom of speech and assembly, insisted that workers should be free to form unions and other voluntary associations, saw world peace as a consequence of free trade, opposed slavery and spoke out against Britain's intervening on behalf of the South in the American Civil War, and worked steadily to extend the right to vote and to make the House of Commons a completely representative body. If these things were known, there would be less inclination among those outside economics to think of it, if at all, as an apologetic, dull and incomprehensible, and less inclination to show surprise on finding something humane and literate in a work about the subject. And there also might be less inclination for economists to respond to the misconception by pursuing their elegant isolation.

4. Once Mill had stated his theory of policy, he made possible a modification of liberalism that was to have important results. He tried to put together two sets of ideas—one came from the classic liberalism of the seventeenth century and directed policy toward increasing the freedom of the individual and protecting his rights; the other came from utilitarianism and directed policy toward improving the individual. Classical economics had harbored both sets of ideas for nearly a century. They had not gotten in each other's way, because no one had tried to define the place of each. Mill tried to make policy serve both freedom and improvement, but in the end he made the latter, the utilitarian objective, the more important. It justifies forms of

intervention that cannot be justified by classic liberalism. The latter was not opposed to intervention per se, but to its being decided independently of the popular will. After Mill made his statement, the liberal tradition was more noticeably divided into two parts: one part continuing the early and classic ideas of liberalism, and the other enlarging upon his ideas, although often unaware of their origin. Utilitarianism led to a policy of extensive government direction, always in the name of liberalism. Both the policy and its name have pained those who remain in the classic tradition, or in what they believe it to be. Who are the genuine liberals? The question is not, Who better represents liberalism?, because liberalism has two distinct components. It really is a question of who is entitled to the name. By antiquity, those in the classic tradition are, because their ideas are somewhat older. The more important question is whose objectives are preferable? That became the issue in the nineteenth century (and remains the issue today).

5. During the century there was substantial opposition to economic liberalism. The opposition was an acknowledgment of its power. In the first half of the century, the target was Ricardian economics, "that canker of states," as one critic called it. The opponents were many of them uninformed, unreasoning, and anachronistic. They were not simply against Ricardo's economics, which few of them understood well enough to criticize. They were opposed to the world it was meant to explain and direct. They were opposed to industrialism and technological change, in their entirety and in each of their aspects, as the M. P. was who said it could not matter less to the nation that the building of railroads would reduce the time needed to transport goods. They were personally offended by the doctrine of overpopulation. Malthus was a *bête noir*. They not only condemned his doctrine but managed somehow to hold him responsible for the danger it described. When they were bold enough to declare what kind of a world they did want (which Burke was too canny to do), it was a mythical, merry, and rather foolish England. Who were these

critics? For the most part their names are unremembered.
One finds their attitude among the memoirs of the period,
in the Parliamentary debates, in the newspapers, and in
the novels. Cobbett sometimes expressed it, and even Dis-
raeli. Despite their anonymity, they deserve notice. They
expressed an attitude that is appealing, enduring, and consequential. It is an attitude of anticapitalism and, more bas-
ically, one that expresses opposition to individualism. It is
found in the twentieth century as well as in the nineteenth,
in such diverse figures as D. H. Lawrence, Ezra Pound,
and Colin Wilson.

Many of the attitudes were stated in cogent form by
Carlyle and Ruskin, and later by an impressive number of
writers and artists, among them William Morris, the Pre-
Raphaelites, and at times, Matthew Arnold. They were political idealists and hence rejected the first premise of liberalism, which is the right and the ability of the individual to
make choices. They made articulate the opposition of the
anonymous critics, and although the ideas were no less atavistic they were stated in a more influential way. The at-
tack on liberalism, made by Carlyle, Ruskin and others like
them, was more consequential, it can be argued, than that
of any other group, more even than that of the Marxists,
who in any event came later.

The working-class opposition to liberalism came from a
different source and it too was earlier than Marxism. It
came first from Robert Owen and the utopian beliefs of
those associated with him. Their doctrine was slight, but it
had great practical effect, notably in the field of cooperatives. Moreover, some of Owen's ideas stung the Ricardians. To read only about how the Ricardians felt toward
the doctrine of Owen is to get the impression of something
quite absurd. It was not that at all. Shortly after Owen began propagating his ideas there developed a socialist version of Ricardian economics, expressed by writers like
Piercy Ravenstone and Thomas Hodgskin. They drew
what seems to be the obvious ethical conclusion from Ricardo's theory of value: If labor produces whatever value a
commodity has, the commodity clearly belongs to labor. It

is interesting that no one seems to have asked why those who produce wealth are entitled to it. Had the question been raised it probably would have been thought foolish. Yet it is not. If those who produce wealth are entitled to it, then those who do not produce are entitled to nothing. If the latter rule had been practiced, a good part of the population would have perished because it consisted of people who owned nothing that produced wealth (children, the aged, the infirm, the indigent, and women). Actually the ethical judgment that was read from the labor theory of value was a judgment that goes far back into history, back beyond Locke and Hobbes to the Old Testament, Genesis, and the idea of original sin—that our bread is the reward of our labor and our labor is the punishment for our disobedience.

There were still others who were opposed to liberalism or to some aspects of it. They were the middle-class and working-class radicals who were not socialists, not atavistic, and not political idealists. They had few ideas of economic policy, but they had a great many policies. The particular object of their opposition was Ricardian economics in certain of its features. They objected to its not recognizing altruism where altruism was a fact; they objected when the Ricardians proposed laisser faire for some markets and they objected when it was *not* proposed for others. They were not in favor of completely free labor markets and were one of the principal forces in support of the Factory Acts. But in international trade they wanted laisser faire established completely and immediately and they would have none of the qualifications to free trade that the Ricardians accepted. Their opposition was much different from that which others expressed toward Ricardian economics. The radical opposition was qualified, good-tempered, and friendly at heart. The ideas on which it acted were liberal ideas. But the radicals were not principally men of ideas at all. They were campaigners, agitators, propagandists, activists. They were also impatient. When Ricardian doctrine counseled them to be moderate, watchful, and patient—they swept it aside.

6. Liberalism had to contend with quite serious economic problems as well as with doctrinal opposition. The depression of 1819 initiated a cyclical movement that has continued ever since and is unlike the irregular and spasmodic fluctuations prior to the nineteenth century. There were severe depressions in the 1840s, 1870s, and 1890s. Early in its history the cycle acquired an international aspect. In the 1830s, the deflationary measures of President Jackson were one cause of the contraction in Britain—probably the first instance of the exporting of unemployment by the United States. Monopolies were another problem. Before the nineteenth century most of them originated in the grant of exclusive rights by the state. Now they originated in the market, and the classical remedy for them was thereby weakened. The remedy had been, particularly in Smith, to abolish government protection of firms and to allow the market to force them to be competitive. Now it was the harshness of competition itself that was a cause of monopoly.

Still another problem was the growing, or apparently growing, inequality of wealth and income. One aspect was the squalor and brutality of the factory towns, and another was the conditions of work in the factories. Actually the average real income of factory workers and their families was almost certainly higher than that of agricultural laborers. There is other evidence that the industrial growth of the century produced more than the wretchedness for which it is notorious. But squalor and brutality were easily seen and readily imputed to the market. The problem was in fact more complex. One of its causes is the inability of a free market to include in the cost of producing manufactured goods all the incidental effects that manufacturing produces, or, in technical language, the inability of a market always to account for social as well as private cost.

Even if the market had been able to reckon all costs there would have remained another problem. It was the most serious of all. It was the quality of the civilization that capitalism was creating. Men still believed that individual economic conduct contributed to the building of character, but after the middle of the century they began to think there were aspects of character that it neglected. Economic individualism certainly is favorable to the development of self-reliance, diligence, reliability, prudence, a respect for facts, and a form of courage that, however rough and simple, is admirable. But individualism also directs one's attention to values that are measurable in money and away from those that are not. Usually those that are not measurable in money are those that matter more: those that are in the arts, in imaginative literature, in the search for knowledge as a thing in itself, that are in the feelings people have for each other and in their sense of what is happy and fitting. They are values that are hard to describe, still harder to communicate, and nearly impossible to appraise. They are not ideas about which demonstrable propositions can be made, as they can be made about many of the ideas in economics. But they are what most men always have thought to be important, and only the foolish or the boorish have turned away from them. This is the problem—the problem of noneconomic values—that brought Carlyle and Ruskin to economics. It made Ruskin deny the premise from which Mill had begun his *Principles.* Mill had said, innocently, that wealth consists of those things measurable in money. "There is no wealth but life," Ruskin thundered (as or nearly as he could in the prose he wrote) and in time he was listened to.[1] This problem has not much interested the Marxists—the other great opponents of liberalism—although they have alluded to it. With the benefit of hindsight, one can see that Marxism was as prosaic in its origins as Ricardian economics was and in practice has turned out to be more materialistic.

For these reasons the nineteenth century was important in the history of economic liberalism, and I wish to bring these studies to a conclusion by describing that period. The information is drawn from what was written and done in Great Britain, because liberalism was more important there than it was in any other country. Other countries had some experience with it, but not in so significant a way. In fact when the nineteenth century is recalled as the age of the

free market, Great Britain, and very little more, is what is
remembered. That little is curious: the tariff reforms of the
autocratic Napoleon III, the free-trade proposals of the
slave owners in the United States, and the enthusiasm for
laisser faire in the court of Tsar Alexander. Laisser faire has
made some disreputable friends and to its embarrassment
continues to do so.

In this chapter I wish specifically: (1) To state the principal measures of policy enacted in Britain to about 1860.
They help to explain the writing on policy, some of which
was about particular enactments, and they show the influence of that writing. By 1860 the direction of government
action was clear and was fixed on a course that did not
change in any important way until after World War I.
(2) To describe the ideas of policy put forward by the
economists, the ways in which the ideas were ambiguous
and needed to be clarified, and the effort of John Stuart
Mill to make a comprehensive statement of the principles
of liberal economic policy. (3) To offer a principle that
seems to me to reconcile the diverse and apparently contradictory elements of liberal policy both in its ideological
and its factual aspects—a principle that integrates both the
ideas of the economists and the enactments of the state. I
propose a new principle because the usual principles do
not seem to be as explanatory.

2 The Practice of Policy

MEASURES THAT PROMOTED THE MARKET

During the century many measures directly or indirectly
promoted free markets and gave the century its reputation
for laisser faire (using that term always to mean nonintervention). One of the first, an indirect measure, was the restoration of the gold standard in 1819. It was the outcome
of the Bullionist controversy of 1810-11, one of the great
debates in the history of economic policy. Those who
wanted to restore gold were most of them economic liberals. But except in international trade, they were not neces-

sarily advocates of laisser faire. Throughout the century
the liberals, and especially the free traders among them,
were in favor of the gold standard and other hard-money
measures. The opponents of hard money usually were pro-
tectionists and were nonliberal on other issues of economic
policy also. Yet on such a basic political issue as Parliamentary reform they agreed with the economic liberals, and
both believed it should be advanced in a radical way. The
division was personified by Richard Cobden and Thomas
Attwood. Attwood stood for protection, paper money, and
Birmingham hardware, while Cobden represented free
trade, gold, and Manchester textiles (the last without enthusiasm). But both were for Parliamentary reform. An interesting feature of the restoration of gold in 1819 was the
behavior of Peel, a Tory, who sponsored it. In 1811 he had
voted against the recommendations of the Bullion Report
to restore gold, but in 1819 he incorporated them in his
own bill. He explained that he hadn't read the report until
1819 and thereupon was persuaded by it. He was to have
another swift change of mind with even more remarkable
consequences. That was in 1845, when he abruptly changed
his opinion about the Corn Laws and sponsored their repeal.

In 1827 another step was taken toward free international
trade. Huskisson, another Tory, inaugurated a program of
tariff reform. Protection was to be limited to 30 percent
and, it was said at the time, might someday be removed
altogether. That is what did happen with the repeal of the
Corn Laws and the Navigation Acts.

There were additional measures that promoted laisser
faire in domestic or international markets. The Combination Acts were repealed in 1824. They had made trade unions illegal and were the major restraint upon the formation of voluntary organizations by the workers. The usury
laws were repealed in 1826. Like the Navigation Acts
they had been napproved eve by Smith, causing Bentham
to challenge him on the point and apparently to change
Smith's mind. There was a drastic revision of the poor laws
in 1834. The change was meant to end the practice of sup-

plementing the wages of agricultural laborers with money from the relief funds. It also intended to make confinement in a workhouse the condition of receiving relief. In 1844 a general law of incorporation was passed, and it removed the necessity of a firm's securing a charter by specific act of Parliament. The granting of monopoly rights by the government was brought to an end. The East India Company, the greatest of the trading monopolies and the creature of government, was abolished in 1858. One of the principal employes who was thereby retired was John Stuart Mill. Each of these measures was the last step in the movement toward making a particular market free. At the time, some of the measures seemed to be an abrupt reversal of policy, such as the restoration of gold and the repeal of the Corn Laws. But in retrospect one can see that prior to each enactment there had been a sequence of events leading to it. This means that when a free market was established, the decision to do so was not made lightly or unexpectedly. The Statute of Apprentices was repealed in 1814. It was a massive piece of legislation that in 1563 gave the government of Elizabeth comprehensive control over the economy. Had it been enforced until 1814 its repeal would have been momentous, but in fact the enforcement began to diminish after 1688, and the repeal was a formality.

While these changes were being made, they were reinforced by others of a political kind. Together the two increased the freedom of the individual to make decisions, the one in the market and the other in political affairs, although neither kind of enactment necessarily provided the individual with the means of using his freedom. Examples of the political changes were the abolition of the slave trade, the abolition of slavery in the British colonies, and the removal of limitations on the political rights of Catholics and Jews. The Reform Bill of 1832 had an economic effect because it gave business interests some of the representation they wanted in the House and so enabled them to propose measures that, by the middle of the century, were meant to establish free markets.

When all such measures are brought together—and others, of an opposite intention or simply of a different intention are ignored—they do suggest that laisser faire governed the century. The suggestion is strengthened by other things about the period that are well remembered, such as the faith in material progress and the satisfaction with it, the collection of virtues which we know of as Victorian morality, the extension of Darwinism into a social philosophy, the miscellany of notions gotten in the novels from *Mary Barton* to the *Forsyte Saga*. There are Carlyle's definitions of classical economics and laisser faire, even more alarming in French: *la science sinistre* and *l'anarchie avec le gendarme en plus*. Just as apposite, though not so familiar, are Cobbett on the Ricardians: "the nasty feelosofers"; Michael Sadler on them: "the pests of society and persecutors of the poor"; and Henry Adams on John Stuart Mill: "His Satanic free-trade majesty."

All of this can lead one to believe that Britain must have been under the rule of the free market and its apologists, as if the idea of laisser faire had taken hold of the country about 1776, when *The Wealth of Nations* was published, and informed it with a grand design that was executed in the next century. The idea is not a simple mistake and is not just a misreading by the twentieth century of what happened in the nineteenth. One can go to the worthies of the nineteenth century and find them expressing the same misconception. No less a one than Cairnes was mistaken. He stated that Britain in his day was ruled by laisser faire and that the majority of the people had an "absolute faith" in it. If it had been his faith also, one could explain his mistake as wishfulness. But it was not. He was in fact intensely opposed to it. Much of what has been said against it in this century was anticipated by him in his celebrated lecture on it in 1870. He said:

Or, turning from particular examples to broad results, can anyone seriously consider the present condition of the inhabitants of these islands—these islands where industrial freedom has for nearly half a century had greater scope than in any previous age or in any other country, but where also the extremes of

wealth and poverty are found in harsher contrast than they have
been ever found elsewhere; where one man consumes more
value in a single meal than goes to feed and clothe the family
of another for a month; where the entire land of the country is
owned by less than a hundred thousand persons out of a population of thirty millions; where one in every twenty persons is a
pauper; where the great bulk of the agricultural population look
forward with calm resignation to spending their old age in a
workhouse; while the artisan population of the towns find themselves about once in ten years in the midst of a frightful commercial catastrophe, which consigns hundreds of thousands to
ruin—I ask if any one can seriously consider this state of things,
and yet repose in absolute satisfaction and confidence on his
maxim of laissez-faire? [2]

The quotation is instructive in two ways. It shows that
the informed as well as the world at large have been mistaken about laisser faire. And it indicates some of the problems—inequality and unemployment—that turned Britain
away from completely free markets and made policy different from what Cairnes supposed it to be. He was, one may
observe, a minor figure in the classical school but not an in-
consequential one. The intensity of the lecture shows that
he looked on the problems of his day as serious problems
indeed. In this he was not alone. The economists were not
indifferent to suffering, and they did not look at it with
the cool detachment that today is thought to be the
proper scientific manner. If they resemble anyone, they
were like the activists of the present: the economists of today who have become personally engaged in the issues of
the time, who have declared their political allegiance, and
have used their skill to justify their political commitments
and to advance them. Today the activists are more likely
not to be in the liberal tradition as the term is used here.

Cairnes' mistake was not unusual. Economists often have
been poor historians, just as historians have been poor economists. Both at times have taken the form of things to be
their substance. Smith (as noted earlier) was one of the
worst offenders. The men who wrote the American Constitution thought they were following the British example
when they divided power among three branches of govern-

ment. Montesquieu had described the British practice in this way, and they had read him diligently. Actually Britain by that time had departed from the practice and had established cabinet government. Another instance is the conception entertained today about the meaning of economic liberalism. The character of that mistake I leave to the reader to ponder after he finishes this book.

MEASURES THAT RESTRICTED THE MARKET

While Britain in the nineteenth century was enacting measures on the principle that the market knows best which goods to produce and how to distribute them, it was at the same time enacting measures on exactly the opposite principle—that the market does not know. It also was enacting a third group of measures that were based on neither principle entirely, but on elements of each. The government taxed personal income during the Napoleonic Wars and retained the power after they were over, using it again in 1842 to restore the revenue lost by the reduction of import duties. The revenue bill of that year was characteristic of the way the political leaders combined principles of policy that seem to be contradictory. By lowering tariffs, the government gave consumers more freedom of choice in the spending of their income. But the government simultaneously levied a direct tax and left them with less income to spend. A later generation would say the net effect was liberalizing, because direct taxes restrict choice less than indirect taxes. The men who made the revenue law may have been familiar with that distinction, but they did not justify their behavior by it. What directed them was the need to make a concession to the free-trade movement and at the same time to find an alternative source of revenue.

The building of the canals and later of the railways had the effect of widening the domestic market and of making it more competitive. The construction was done mainly by private enterprise, although an exception was the Caledonian Canal in Scotland. Bentham approved of the government's building it while M'Culloch said the money was "little better than thrown away." Unlike the governments on the Continent, that of Britain wanted neither to own the transportation systems nor to give them subsidies. However, it did not scruple to regulate certain technical aspects of construction (such as the gauge of the railways), to specify the routes, to control the competition between canals and railways, to regulate the consolidation of the latter, and, most important, to fix rates. The Combination Acts were repealed in 1824, as stated above, and the government thereby accepted the principle of voluntary association. But there followed a number of laws defining permissible trade-union activity, the first of them passed the very next year and continuing to the arbitration law of 1896.

That the government was responsible for maintaining employment was not a novel idea in the nineteenth century —it was indeed thought to be reactionary and even archaic. When expressly put before the House in 1848 it was repudiated.[3] Still, in 1863 a law was passed that empowered certain public agencies to borrow money in order to provide work for the unemployed or to make direct payments to them. The law clearly was inconsistent with the New Poor Law of 1834. Moreover, in the thirty intervening years there had been no softening of the dogma that charity was unwise. Charity, men believed, was demoralizing because it made the poor dependent and lazy. After 1859, when *The Origin of the Species* was published, the notion was reinforced by the belief that protecting the weak makes for the survival of the unfit. Actually Britain was well prepared, verbally, to apply Darwinism to social behavior. Mill, for example, had proposed to help the poor by making the receipt of relief so onerous that they would be driven to supporting themselves. He seems not to have been influenced directly by Darwin but he was quite familiar with the ideas of Spencer who was. In any event, he made the proposal eleven years before Darwin's work was published. And he himself made the best comment on his own proposal in *On Liberty*, where he said a characteristic of the English is to assert an outrageous principle long after they have given up any intention of practicing it.

The idea that prices and the quality of goods should be controlled was repudiated in the same way as the idea that the government was responsible for maintaining employment. Both ideas were Elizabethan and authoritarian, it was said. Yet the repudiation was contravened by a number of laws, beginning in 1825 with one that provided for the inspection of the food supply. As illuminating gas, then electricity, the telegraph, and the telephone came into being, the government controlled their rates and nationalized the latter two.

In monetary policy, one of the major laws was the Bank Charter Act of 1844, again sponsored by Peel, the major craftsman of economic policy of the century. It was a complex piece of legislation, and in its entirety cannot be described as promoting either laisser faire or the opposite. It prevented the joint-stock banks from issuing paper money and provided that no new rights of issue be given to private banks in the future. In time the joint-stock banks absorbed the private banks, and that left the Bank of England with a monopoly of the right of issue. Cobden supported the monopoly because the conditions of issue were fairly consistent with the gold standard. Mill did not see any importance in the question of monopoly versus competition in the issue of currency. The act did not alter a law of 1826 which had abolished the Bank of England's monopoly of joint-stock banking. Actually the major economic issue in the debate over the Charter Act was how to regulate the supply of money, and on that issue there were liberal and nonliberal economists on each side.

There was another important aspect of monetary policy, and it deserves more notice than it has received. The government, when business firms were in financial distress, guaranteed loans made to them by commercial banks. The Treasury issued Exchequer Bills to the firms, which in turn used their inventories as collateral; the firms then discounted the bills and increased their cash holdings. The purpose was to prevent forced sales of goods and to arrest a deflationary movement. The practice had started in the eighteenth century and always was much favored by businessmen, including those who favored a laisser faire solution to other problems. During the depression of 1836-37 the merchants and manufacturers of Manchester petitioned the government to reform the Corn Laws. The effect, they thought, would be to increase their exports (their argument being that a lower tariff on grain would cause Britain to import more of it, thereby providing foreigners with more British money which would be spent on British goods). In making the proposal, the business community also made some ringing declarations for the principle of free markets. At the same time it asked the government to issue Exchequer Bills. They had been a point in the Bullionist controversy, the gold standard people having opposed them. But their reason was not that the issue of bills was a form of government intervention. It was that the bills increased the monetary instability caused by the suspension of gold payments and contributed to the excessive profits of the Bank of England.

Laws that altered the distribution of income by taxing it, that tried to make transportation more efficient and fairly priced by intervening in its construction and the setting of its rates, that tried to regulate trade unions, settle labor disputes, support employment, fix prices, control the quality of food, that nationalized some public utilities, established a monopoly of the issue of paper money, that tried to prevent deflationary movements—such laws do not support the belief expressed by Cairnes, and many others then and since, that laisser faire was the governing policy of the country and the absolute faith of the majority of the people.

Beyond these laws, older than most of them and more consequential than any, was another form of intervention. It was the regulation of working conditions by the Factory Acts. The stated purpose of the acts was to reduce the hours of work, and that was their direct effect. But indirectly they raised hourly wages. That both changes would occur was recognized quite early, but the acts were not offered by their sponsors as a means of controlling wages. They were in their initial stage not even presented as a means of improving the condition of the laboring classes, except by a

few radical businessmen like Owen and workers like David
Brook. The first was passed in 1802. The purpose was to
make the government attend to its obligations to apprentices, a responsibility it had been given by the Elizabethan
Poor Law of 1601. The act of 1802 applied to the textile industry. Among other things, it required the mill owners to
provide some education for the children in their employment. Education was also a feature of subsequent acts. In
time the state regulated the conditions of work of all children in the textile mills (not just orphan apprentices), then
extended regulation to the working conditions of women,
then to the working conditions of both women and children
outside the textile industry, and finally to men. At the end
of the century most of the working population outside agriculture was within the scope of the acts. By then the acts
were accepted as much by the descendants of the Manchester school as by the admirers of Lord Ashley, an early
sponsor. With similar feelings, both could look back on the
early opposition to the laws. It was like that stated in the
following excerpt from the minutes of a Select Committee
of 1816, appointed by Parliament to examine the proposal
to improve the condition of workers:

  Is the condition of the people generally comfortable, and are
  they themselves happy and contented?—They are generally so,
  as far as I know; if they are not happy, they can leave it.[4]

That is laisser faire of a purity that is primordial. It is
what is supposed to have been common in the nineteenth
century. But the Factory Acts were passed, and so were
others that modified free markets or eliminated them altogether. There were many more than are noted here. Spencer in 1880 listed several scores.[5] But they were less important and do not alter the point I wish to make—that the
policy of Britain in the century was a combination of measures, some promoting free markets, some with the opposite
intention, and a third group (like the Exchequer Bills)
that mixed the two.

THE INFLUENCE OF PARTIES AND INTERESTS

How can the policy be explained, and what shall it be called? Is there a principle to be read from it? Or was it the work of party politics, or of vested interests?

One explanation is that it was all of these things, because, in this view, policy is politics and politics by its nature cannot be consistent (or more than superficially so). The policy of the nineteenth century is looked upon as a collection of diverse measures, each meant to manage a particular problem in whatever way it could be managed: by using some principle or other of economic policy, by the party in power enacting something from its program, or by the government yielding to the pressure of a vested interest. But this is not really an explanation, because it says that what happened is not to be explained in any one way.

What can be said of party behavior as an explanation? The Whigs were associated with economic individualism, freedom of contract, and similar notions ascribed to liberalism, while the Tories were associated with protection for agriculture, a hostility to trade, and a state of mind that disliked the market and its works. But these associations were so flexible, were so often qualified and even contradicted, that they are not helpful as explanations. Let me cite just two facts. Most of the measures here noted—and they were the most important—were approved by majorities in the House in excess of the majority held by the party in office when the laws were passed. The other fact is that when the main features of the policy were established —in the years from 1819 to 1846, between the resumption of gold convertibility and the establishment of free trade in grain—the leading economic statesman was Peel. He promoted measures that cannot be connected with the program of either party any more than they can be connected with laisser faire or its opposite. From the political historians, Peel has received the attention he merits. But the economists have not been as attentive. They are inclined to think it was Gladstone or Robert Lowe who made the critical decisions about policy and gave the century its distinctive features. Gladstone and Lowe are best remembered for some high-minded statements in favor of laisser faire. Yet neither *acted*, as distinct from spoke, as though he wanted the principle to guide the state. Actually, before they came to power the course of policy had been pretty firmly established by Peel.

How influential were vested interests? They certainly did have influence, but it was not strong or consistent enough to make it the explanation of policy. There were indeed times when Parliament acted as if it wanted to prove it was the official representative of the bourgeoisie. At the time of the Bullion controversy the House heard the petition of the cotton textile workers for relief in the depression of 1811. They wanted a law to limit the number of apprentices. They could not have it, they were told, because the House would not legislate against laisser faire. The point was made strongly by Perceval and Rose, two leaders of the anti-Bullionist group, who were joined by Giddy, a Bullionist. The Members also expressed opposition to the granting of money to the poor, which, they said, was wholly objectionable.

The government at the time was making loans to employers. The workers were turned away in June of that year, and in November the Luddite riots began. In the 1830s the House turned away the handloom weavers when they petitioned for help to relieve their technological unemployment. They were told the House had no power to change the laws of economics. At the same time it listened to the businessmen who asked for (and received) loans to carry their inventories. The textile manufacturers at times acted as if they were illustrating some of the cruder doctrines of imperialism. They repeatedly called on the Foreign Office to use influence and if necessary military power to open foreign markets to them, as when in 1848 they demanded the lifting of the Danish blockade of the Elbe so that cotton goods could be shipped to Germany.

There are, however, far too many examples of the opposite sort of thing, and they cast overwhelming doubt on the notion that policy was the work of vested interests. The

Foreign Office often refused the exporters' requests. Parliament took almost forty years to repeal the Corn Laws. On the great issue of regulating the conditions of work, it acted in opposition to the majority of employers. When one looks into the origin of laws that were detrimental to business, or were thought to be by the business community, one finds they often were promoted by a few unusual businessmen. The Factory Acts are a good example. I am not saying that vested interests on the whole were indifferent to what Parliament did, or that they did not try to use Parliament for their purposes. They often tried and sometimes succeeded. But they did not use political power as often as its use was called for, and when they did, their behavior often was inept and fearful, and they did not often succeed.

These remarks—about the influence of parties and interests—are not offered as conclusive evidence. The reader interested in the point will want much more. To supply it would take me much beyond the purpose of this chapter which is to explain what determined policy and to treat only incidentally of what did not. I believe that a detailed historical study would support the statements I have made.

3 The Meaning of Economic Liberalism

What determined policy in the nineteenth century was, in my opinion, ideas, and the ideas in their entirety constitute economic liberalism. They were long in developing, as the period of time covered by this book indicates, and when they came to be a full-bodied doctrine it was not a simple or self-evident one. Some of the ideas were fairly explicit propositions that had been made in the writings of the economists and transferred to government enactments. Free trade is an example and it is an example of laisser faire, which was one element of liberalism but not the most important. Some of the other elements were inferences drawn by the economists from what the government actually had done. The regulation of factory labor is an example and it illustrates the idea that some markets should be controlled. Still other elements were the combined product of the observation of economists and the work of political leaders, each looking at a problem from their particular viewpoints, but influencing each other and in the end coming to agreement. Poor relief is an example. These ideas cannot be made consistent in any obvious way. To do that one must go beyond economics and into political philosophy.

Liberal economic policy is deduced from the political principle that free people may do what they will do and are able to do. The statement is abstract, possibly vague and even sententious, but I do not know of any other way to state the principle briefly. What I mean by it is this: (1) A measure of policy to be liberal must be a response to an economic problem which the people believe should be attended to. (2) The measure must be workable, that is, must show some likelihood of being able to solve the problem to which it is directed. (3) The methods it uses must be approved by the people. By "the people," I mean those persons who are represented in government, whose opinion the government must take for its guide, and who in the end control the government. Their number increased in the nineteenth century, because the franchise was extended and other democratic changes were made. In the eighteenth century, representative government was much more limited. In the twentieth, where it exists, it is more extensive in the sense that more adults are able to vote, electoral districts are represented more nearly in proportion to their population, civil liberties are more universal, and (though hard to believe perhaps) government is less corrupt. Over this period, economists in the tradition of classic liberalism have moved farther from laisser faire and toward more intervention. The movement is, I believe, causally related to the extension of representative government. Where government is by the few, individuals cannot express their choices by means of it, except with great difficulty. In such circumstances the market is a better means. No matter how unequally income may be distributed, and other power as well, the market is impersonal and in the aggregate is predictable. But where government represents the many, it can be a means by which individuals express their choices. It can keep before itself the ideal rule of policy making, which is to obtain for an action the consent of those affected by it. An ideal market also does just that. But private-social cost discrepancies and other limitations prevent markets from being ideal. If such limitations are remediable, they need not, in a representative state, be borne. The people, without jeopardizing their liberties, can direct the government to intervene. The limitations may not be remediable. Obviously that is reason enough for the government not to intervene. But the reason is a mechanical, not an ethical, one. It applies with equal force in a dictatorship.

INTERVENTION AND DEMOCRACY

To say that intervention and democracy developed together in the history of liberalism is not the same as saying that where one is, the other will be found also. Today the countries where government intervenes most are those in which there is least democracy, namely, the Communist countries. What the connection between democracy and intervention means is this: Among countries with representative government today, those which by almost every test provide the greatest political liberty for the individual are also those where the state has intervened most. Examples are Scandinavia and Great Britain. Where the political liberty of the individual is less secure, as I believe it to be in the United States, there is less intervention—and, from a liberal viewpoint, properly so. There is an interesting confirmation of the connection in the Communist countries today. In the writings of some of their economists there are proposals for less intervention and more reliance on the market.[6] The reason is that a Communist government, being unrepresentative, cannot discern the choices of individuals. That is a serious failing because even a dictatorial government needs to be guided by individual choices in some matters, such as the composition of consumer output. In other words, where government is bad, whether it is an oligarchy in Britain in the eighteenth century or a "people's democracy" in eastern Europe in the twentieth, individuals can get what they want better through the market. To be accurate, it must be said that the Communists who propose the market do so as a means of improving the efficiency of the economy and not as a means of increasing individual freedom. But that is dust in our eyes, because they implicitly measure efficiency by the way the economy responds to individual choices. Otherwise they wouldn't propose it be directed by them. Should the Communist countries put the proposal into complete effect, they probably will lessen their political dictatorship, because the need for much of the dictatorship will be removed. We then might see democracy brought into being by laisser faire, as in the West for many years we have seen democracy bring intervention into being—an instance of the dialectic indeed. It is irresistible to speculate about what will happen when the movements intersect: when the West in its movement toward intervention meets the east in its movement toward laisser faire. What then will be the allegiance of the orthodox Marxists, and where will the disciples of von Mises find a home?

WHAT LIBERAL POLICY IS NOT

This much, then, for what the principle of liberal economic policy is. It is, to repeat, that government *may* do whatever it *can* do that the people *will have* it do. Consider what it does not mean. It does not mean that policy must be based on consensus. That very useful word I prefer to use to mean unanimous agreement. That can be taken as the ideal and limiting standard of policy, the measure of absolute popular will, and the goal toward which we should move. But reaching the goal—which means achieving unanimity—cannot be a necessary condition of enacting policy. That is so for two reasons. The practical reason is that unanimity is impossible on most issues, or it is unnecessary, or it takes too long to obtain. Problems are pressing, and solutions must be reached. To make consensus a condition of solving problems is to leave them unsolved, which can be a very expensive practice—as it would be, for example, if

the government did nothing about maintaining employment until everyone approved of the thing to be done. The
other reason is that government by consensus is a contradiction in terms. Government is coercion and is unnecessary
where there is unanimity. People do not have to be coerced
into doing something they freely choose to do. To *strive*
for consensus is a commendable thing and a necessary
thing, just as striving for virtue is commendable and necessary. I do not write ironically. But to insist upon *achieving*
both is, in practice, to reduce behavior to ineffectuality
and, in theory, to produce a contradiction. A religious man
sensibly can say we should seek to be angelic as a condition of entering heaven, but to insist that we actually be so
is to say that we shall enter heaven only when earth has become like it. A liberal sensibly can say that government
should have the consent of as many as possible when it
takes action. But for him to say government must have the
consent of everyone is to say it should act as if governing
were not necessary.

THE NECESSARY AMOUNT OF AGREEMENT

We come next to the question of how much consent or
agreement there should be. That depends, it seems to me,
on the importance of the measure and on the length of
time during which it is being argued or has been in effect.
An important measure obviously should command more
support just because it affects more people or affects them
more deeply. There are ways of sensing what is more and
what is less important. If a proposed measure evokes sharp
differences, if it agitates the public, it probably is important
and does not have sufficient support to justify its being enacted, even though it may have a nominal majority in the
legislature. But these observations must be qualified. Controversy can be manufactured, and there will seem to be
less agreement than there actually is. Even when real, the
controversy may be ephemeral. It is the business of the
legislature to decide what is in the public interest in the long
run. Its business is not to be guided by the opinion of the
moment. If it is wrong about the public interest, the public

will correct it at the next election. There can be circumstances in which it legitimately can enact a measure that
clearly is against what the public at the time believes to be
in its interest. The legislature may do so if it believes the
public will change its view once it has experience with
the measure. If, however, the opposition is continued, or if
the measure is difficult to enforce, or if the public refuses to
return to office those who enacted it, then the measure
should be repealed. Repeal can be very difficult to effect.
Hence it is prudent to reduce the scope of a controversial
measure and use it to make marginal rather than fundamental changes. If this is impossible, the measure should
not be enacted, and the legislature simply must wait until
there is public approval.

These remarks about agreement are not precise, and
some readers will be dissatisfied with them. What I am
saying is that the amount of agreement necessary for the
enactment of a measure of liberal policy is that amount
which the legislature judges to be necessary. Therefore it
is the judgment of legislators that decides what is and what
is not consistent with the popular will. There are many who
do not care for legislators. Some do not because they are
opposed to representative government and not simply to
the legislators who carry it on. The issue between them and
me is not whether the legislature can interpret the popular
will. The issue is whether popular will should guide policy,
or whether policy should be guided by some impersonal
force like history, a divine will, natural law, a racial spirit,
or even a force like an enlightened few who believe they
know what is good for the population better than the population itself knows. Those who oppose the popular will are
simply opposed to liberalism in its most fundamental aspect.

There is another group of people. They subscribe to
liberalism, but have little confidence in legislators. That is
because they have little confidence in government per se.
They can marshal evidence of what Spencer called the
sins of legislators. But the evidence proves too much—
namely, that government should not exist at all, or that it

has deprived us of fundamental liberties. The former is not a helpful conclusion, while the latter simply does not correspond to our experience. If it were true that everything the government does, beyond the maintenance of law and order, is an action that deprives individuals of some of their liberty, then we should now feel quite unfree even in normally democratic countries. We should feel restrained by compulsory school laws, public schools themselves, utility regulation, most monetary policies, progressive taxation, and a great many other things that are a common part of our existence. I do not say there can be no reasonable objection to such things. There can be and is. What I am saying is that we do not believe these things place us under restraints that are constantly irksome, chafing, and so objectionable that we would, if we could, throw them off.

THE OBJECTIONS TO INTERVENTION

Actually those who object to these measures do so for three reasons—reasons they do not keep as separate as they should. One is that a particular measure limits the freedom of one group of people for the sake of providing benefits to others, such as the income tax. Is such limitation inconsistent with freedom? Not necessarily. One of the ideas with which classic liberalism began was that government must restrain the exercise of power by individuals in order to make peace and harmony possible among them. There is a great practical difference between the government's preventing the strong from endangering the lives of the weak and its preventing one man from earning more than thirty times as much as another. But I do not see any reason in principle why, if the physical power of an individual may be limited, his income power may not be also. Both violence and inequality produce what can be called (to paraphrase Henry C. Simons) the ugly society. If government may intervene to prevent the one, it may also intervene to prevent the other, always assuming of course that the people want it to do so and it is able to. A second reason for objecting to a measure is that it does not do what it is represented as doing. One example is agricultural legislation that is represented as helping poor farmers while in fact it helps rich farmers much more. But this reason for objecting has nothing to do with the effect of the measure on individual freedom. If it is the unworkability of the measure that makes it objectionable, then a workable measure should be proposed in its place. If not, even a workable measure would be acceptable, because it restrains individuals, then workability is irrelevant. The third reason for objecting is that a measure helps only one group in the population and injures all others, such as a protective tariff. This in my opinion is the most telling objection that can be brought against government intervention. It says that intervention is bad if it sacrifices the interest of many to the interest of a few. But that is not an objection to intervention per se. It is an objection to intervention that contravenes the public will. The objection in fact is quite consistent with the principle I have offered for appraising policy.

I have said nothing about the common view that detailed intervention in the end must destroy freedom. It is the view put forward in so influential a way by Hayek in *The Road to Serfdom*. He states that in a centrally directed economy the claims of efficiency must come before those of freedom. His argument is closely reasoned and deductive. It rests on definitions of intervention and of freedom that lead necessarily to his conclusion. The argument is not, in my opinion, supported by such historical evidence as is relevant to it. What is more important is that the meaning he assigns to liberalism is not the meaning I believe is to be read from the economists whom both of us take to be representatives of the doctrine. This is not the place to comment on the details of his argument, and I wish only to add that with some of them I am in agreement.

ALTERNATIVE CONCEPTIONS OF LIBERALISM

Although the principle I infer from liberalism is not all I would like it to be, I can think of none better. It is more helpful than the principles now used by economists who think of themselves as liberal. For the reason given above, the idea of consensus is just not practicable or consistent.

To alter it to mean majority rule is not satisfactory. To enact measures that have majority support may not be liberal, because the measures may not respect the legitimate interests of minorities. Moreover, the idea of majority rule is of no help at all in understanding the liberalism of the past. During most of the history of liberalism the idea of majority rule was of no consequence as a standard of policy. When the liberals did notice it, they usually made their opposition to it quite clear.

Another approach is to decide whether or not a measure is liberal by some standard other than individual freedom. The standard most often used is efficiency. In this view a measure is liberal, even though it may restrict freedom, if it produces a more efficient and/or a more complete allocation of resources than can be obtained from a free market. For example, government may intervene to maintain full employment, as it does in the exercise of monetary policy, or to equalize private and social costs, as it does in conserving water resources. But efficiency is a siren song, despite the fact that most American economists heed it. To put it in the place of freedom is to open the prospect of an economy of well-regulated penitentiaries in which, as Jacob Viner once said, there is no unemployment or other inefficiency. American economists, of course, do not really believe in putting efficiency before everything else. Like their British colleagues, they are far too good to put into practice what their beliefs imply. But they ought to say just what the limits to efficiency are to be. In doing so they undoubtedly will consider other values also. The objective of their policy probably will be a mixture of individual freedom, efficiency, equality, security, and growth. In deciding on the proportions in the mixture, they will be brought around to considering what the public wants from the economy. In other words, they will be guided by their estimation of the popular will. And in accepting the guidance, they will be acting on the principle that was used by the liberal economists of the past.

4 *The Ideas of Policy*

The writings of the nineteenth century reveal how frequently the liberal economists were guided by their appraisal of the popular will. By this principle the writings became intelligible; and although it does not make them consistent, it does reveal the intent that directed them. If on the other hand the writings are studied for their consistency with laisser faire they disclose as much ambiguity and lack of direction as the practice of policy does. The economists wrote both for and against free markets, and it was not unusual for a single writer to do both. They could be explicit about some measures of policy and obscure about others. On particular problems they could be clear and cogent, while about the principle from which they derived their position they could be superficial, indistinct, or simply silent. They would conform to our notions of British pragmatism if they always had been this way, i.e., attentive to specific solutions and indifferent to the principles they imply. They usually were so about the Factory Acts, declaring themselves for or against a particular act, but not for or against the principle of regulating working conditions. Pragmatism, in this rough and ready sense, is popular among economists today, particularly among those who refuse to commit themselves either to the principle of a free market or to its opposite, and who judge a measure of policy by whether or not it solves the problem to which it is addressed. They do not really believe one solution is as good as another—that, for example, eliminating unemployment by fiscal measures is no better or worse than by forced-labor camps. What they believe is that neither laisser faire nor its opposite is a helpful guide to policy. They believe just what the nineteenth century economists implied that they, too, believed. Unfortunately, neither has been clear about what other principle should guide policy, and the writings of today like those of a century ago often imply there are no other principles.

In the nineteenth century there was uncertainty about the principles of policy. The reason was not pragmatism. The classicists did not ignore principles. They did not attend only to particular problems. They are, in fact, known—and properly so—for doing just the opposite. They wrote of the principle of free foreign trade and usually declared themselves for it. They also wrote about other principles—about what should govern poor relief, the supply of money, the fixing of prices, etc. Beyond this they wrote about the most general of all principles—that which should direct the state in its relation to the economy. What they did *not* do was to explain how the principles were related to each other and to the measures of policy that were derived from them. What they especially failed to do was to explain adequately the most general of the principles, namely the principle on which the state should base its economic policy.

The uncertainty was the signal feature of nineteenth-century liberalism until Mill wrote his *Principles*. It was not, however, a unique feature. It was inherited from the eighteenth century and particularly from Smith. To illustrate the uncertainty, I should like to return to him briefly and to the idea for which he is best known and most misunderstood: the invisible hand. What the idea actually means is, I believe, this: if an individual acts only for himself he *may* do more for others than if he tries to help them or is compelled to help them by the state. I do not take the idea to mean that selfishness always increases the national wealth, or that individuals always are selfish, or that the state never should tell them what to do. It usually is interpreted to mean one or all of these things. But consider its context and the language in which it is stated. It is in Book IV, "Of Systems of political Oeconomy," in Chapter 2, "Of Restraints upon the Importation from foreign Countries of such Goods as can be produced at Home." It follows an examination of the idea that the protection of domestic industries will increase the employment and output of the nation. Smith states that protection "frequently" increases employment in the protected industry. "But whether it tends either to increase the general industry of the society, or to give it the most advantageous direction, is not, perhaps, altogether so evident." It will be noted that Smith did not unequivocally oppose protection; indeed elsewhere in *The Wealth of Nations* he stated he favored it under certain circumstances.

The argument continues that total employment depends on total capital and that total output depends on the efficiency with which capital is used. Efficiency is measured by profit, and a large profit indicates that output is large. Smith assumes here (as he does not everywhere) that every man tries to increase his profit. It follows that every man works to increase total output even though to increase it is no part of his purpose. Whatever the rate of profit is, it is more certain in a domestic than in a foreign enterprise because the businessman can attend more carefully to the capital he has at home. If the two rates are about equal, he will use his capital at home and in a way that seems most profitable to him. If he succeeds, employment will increase at home and output will also, even though his private and exclusive purpose had been to increase profit. Then follows the paragraph in which the famous phrase appears:

But the annual revenue of every society is always precisely equal to the exchangeable value of the whole annual produce of its industry, or rather is precisely the same thing with that exchangeable value. As every individual, therefore, *endeavours* as much as he can both to employ his capital in the support of domestic industry, and so to direct that industry that its produce may be of the greatest value; every individual *necessarily* labours to render the annual revenue of the society as great as he can. He *generally*, indeed, neither intends to promote the public interest, nor knows how much he is promoting it. By preferring the support of domestic to that of foreign industry, he intends only his own security; and by directing that industry in such a manner as its produce may be of the greatest value, he intends only his own gain, and he is *in this, as in many other cases*, led by an invisible hand to promote an end which was no part of his intention. Nor is it *always* the worse for the society that it was no part of it. By pursuing his own interest he *frequently* promotes that of the society more effectually than when he really intends to promote it. I have never known much good done by those who affected to trade for the public good. It is an affectation, indeed, not very common among merchants, and very few words need be employed in dissuading them from it.[7]

The italics I have added are meant to draw attention to the qualifications. Smith stated that everyone "endeavours" to increase profit; he did not say everyone always does increase it. He did not say that the search for profit necessarily increased employment and output, but that it necessarily is an effort to do so. He said men "generally" do not act in the public interest; he did not say they never do. He said that selfishness is "frequently" more beneficial than altruism; he did not say it always is. The context and language make the statement about the invisible hand a statement that expresses qualified opposition to protection. It certainly does not say that laisser faire should be the principle of policy, because it is not even a statement in favor of complete free trade. When it is related to other ideas of policy in the *Wealth of Nations*, it is terribly confusing. Elsewhere the opposition to protective duties is qualified even more. As the reader knows from Chapter 1 in this volume, Smith qualified the idea that individuals try to increase profit and also the idea that when they do they act in the public interest.

With so much ambiguity in *The Wealth of Nations*, the lack of clarity is not surprising in the economists of the nineteenth century. They looked to Smith for direction about policy as they looked to Ricardo for their positive economics.

ON THE PRINCIPLE OF NONINTERFERENCE

The ambiguity was most noticeable in the statements of M'Culloch, whose literal manner revealed aspects of classical economics which the greater minds kept obscure. He was the first professor of political economy at University College of the University of London, a project of the radical Benthamites by which they meant to combat the influence of Oxford and Cambridge. He gave his first two lectures in 1829 and said he proposed "to inquire into the proper bounds of legislative interference with property and trade." *The Morning Chronicle* reported: "The laws, he said, which regulated the prosperity and decay of nations, were as certain as those which govern the celestial bodies; but more interesting, inasmuch as man might modify them by his interferences."

Nevertheless he wrote in his *Principles* that noninterference should be the guide to policy and that exceptions were permissible only when they clearly could be shown to be of public advantage. The control of child labor was one exception, he believed. He was impressed by the testimony against child labor given before the Sadler committee of 1832 (the same Sadler who called the economists the persecutors of the poor) and he supported the Factory Act proposed in 1833. His support is notable because that bill substantially increased the extent of control. He wrote to Lord Ashley, its original sponsor: "I hope your factory bill will prosper and I am glad it is in such good hands. Had I a seat in the House it should assuredly have my vote. A notion is entertained that Political Economists are, in all cases, enemies to all sorts of interference, but I assure you that I am not one of those who entertain such an opinion." He made it plain, however, that he did not approve of the control of adult labor, which some of the bill's supporters hoped would be its eventual outcome. His reason seems to have been the principle of the free agent, which is that individuals should be free to work under whatever conditions they choose. He did not apply it to children, because they do not have "the power to judge for themselves in such a matter." The principle suggests that M'Culloch believed freedom was the major goal of policy. But he wrote again in the *Principles:* "Freedom is not, as some appear to think, the end of government." The end is public prosperity and happiness, and freedom is a means to it and not the only means.[8] Just what was the relationship among the alternative means, and how the means were to be selected to serve the end—he did not make clear, no more than Smith had done before him.

Until 1848 most economists viewed the Factory Acts in the way M'Culloch did. They approved of the control of child labor but not of that of adults. The apparent reason for the distinction was that a child cannot make sensible choices. But I do not believe that was the actual reason. They did not consistently make the distinction and initially did not make it at all. In 1818 Lauderdale in the House of Lords had single-handedly secured the withdrawal of an act regulating child labor on the grounds that "the great principle of Political Economy [is] that labour ought to be left free" [9]—meaning all labor, not just that of adults. As successive acts raised the age at which children could be employed, more and more exceptions were taken to the great principle. When women were brought within the acts the principle was weakened even more. Eventually the acts covered men also, and by that time the principle (in its application to factory legislation) had been completely repudiated. The economists also repudiated other putative principles. Nevertheless the public continued to entertain what M'Culloch called the notion that political economy meant noninterference.

THE REPUTATION FOR PESSIMISM

The notion the public got from Chadwick and Senior was distinctive and deeply felt. It also was wrong. Chadwick, who had been secretary to Bentham, joined Senior in writing the Poor Law in 1834. More than any other measure of policy it gave economics the name of the dismal science. The law prohibited the use of relief funds to supplement the wages of farm laborers (which were pitifully low because agriculture was comparatively inefficient) and it prohibited relief payments to the poor. They could get help only if they entered a workhouse, where they labored at something or other. There, husbands were separated from wives, and both separated from their children. The law certainly was harsh. However, it was not the work of men dedicated to laisser faire. Wage subsidies caused labor to

be misallocated, and relief caused idleness—so it was said
—and these were the evils the act was meant to eliminate.
But it was never completely enforced, and its objects in
time were attained by rising employment. Chadwick became
secretary of the enforcing agency and, to everyone's aston-
ishment, used his authority to increase the welfare activities
of the government. That was the finest irony of the period.
For writing the law he was called heartless, and for ad-
ministering it, sentimental; condemned at first for wanting
to do too little for the poor, he later was condemned for
wanting to do too much. There are several explanations of
the episode. One is that Chadwick changed his mind when
he got to know the poor, sloughed off his laisser faire notions and allowed his natural humanity to express itself.
Another explanation is that the doctrine of Bentham, his
mentor, does not imply laisser faire at all, but its very opposite. I suggest the explanation is that Chadwick, like
other liberals, did what he believed society wanted done—
that, in other words, he acted on the liberal principle.

The explanation applies to Senior also. He wanted the
state to do little, while Chadwick wanted it to do much.
But they differed over what the state was *able* to do and
what it was *wise* in doing, not over what it had the *right*
to do. Senior was on the Royal Commission appointed
in 1837 to study the condition of the handloom weavers.
They were being displaced by power looms and becoming impoverished. The weavers' distress was brought on
by the decline in the demand for their labor, the Commission reported, and went on to advise them to move to
other occupations. Except by assisting in their education,
there was little, the report stated, the government could
do. The report fortified those who believed that political
economy when confronted with human distress made a
sad face, folded its arms, and explained tendentiously that
any effort to improve conditions must make them worse.
"Not an amiable faith," Carlyle remarked, and in the same
spirit someone a century later said, "To hell with economics—let's build a better world." The remarks are really
beside the point. The issue is the factual one of whether

or not the state is *able* to solve certain problems, not whether it has the *right* to do so. The state probably was able to do something for the weavers, just as in fact it did do something for distressed employers at about the same time.

THE FACTUAL ELEMENT IN POLICY

On factual matters the economists were more often wrong than right, and it makes one uncomfortable to notice that the greater mistakes were made over the problems of the poor. The reason was not that their sympathies were with the rich and the well born—it was that they were still in the coils of the reaction to the optimism of the eighteenth century, to Godwin and Condorcet and the vision of a new Eden. Malthus was the first to react, and his pessimism was shared by others, all of them infusing it with the skepticism inherited from Hume and Smith. Malthus was wrong about the population of England, Ricardo was wrong in much the same way in his iron law of wages, and John Stuart Mill was wrong about the national debt (it must be paid before the coal reserves were exhausted, he warned[10]). Nearly everyone was wrong in believing that a generous treatment of the poor would make them lazy. One could compile an impressive catalog of the mistakes of the nineteenth-century economics (though the catalog need not be confined to that period). If they dwell on error, the histories of economics show where it went wrong on points of theory. The two—theory and policy—are related. The economists were mistaken about policy when their theory was wrong or incomplete or just didn't exist. The mistakes came from their science, the positive side of theory and not from their politics or their ethics which is the normative side. Most commentaries suppose classical economic policy was determined by the normative side, or that the two are inseparable. Thus we are told that Senior was an enemy of factory legislation because he, like others, was dedicated to the principle of noninterference.

Not so. Senior was mistaken on a point of positive economics in his celebrated *Letters on the Factory Act,* written about the ten-hour bill that was proposed in 1837 (but passed in a much weakened form). He stated that hourly wages would rise and that output per man-hour would not; that profits would fall and so would employment or real wages. "I have no doubt, therefore, that a ten hours' bill would be utterly ruinous." [11] The argument is much like that of today's opponents of wage-and-hour laws. He certainly was right that hourly wages would rise—because he assumed weekly wages would be constant —but he was not right in stating that output would be constant. It could have increased simply because fewer hours were worked and the workers could put more into each hour. It also could have increased by increasing or improving the capital with which each worker was employed (although that is more an argument for increasing investment than for reducing hours). Both did happen during the century, and they have been harsh on Senior's judgment. But, to repeat, the judgment was factual. It was not a declaration against the right of the state to interfere. Had he thought the facts were otherwise, he undoubtedly would have supported the act of 1837. A few years earlier, before he wrote his unfortunate letters, he had approved of the very important act of 1833. When the letters were put in a second edition he approved of the proposal made in 1841 to restrict child labor still more, and in 1847 he himself proposed still another limitation.

"It is the duty of a Government to do whatever is conducive to the welfare of the governed," he said in his second Oxford lectures, given between 1847 and 1852. "The only limit to this duty is its power. And as the supreme Government of an independent State is necessarily absolute, the only limit to its power is its moral or physical inability. And whatever it is its duty to do it must necessarily have a right to do." This expresses Senior's policy more clearly than his *Letters* do, and the policy was not laisser faire. Indeed, he said, that was "the most fatal of all errors." [12]

Cairnes also believed it to be a great error. His denunciation of it was quoted some pages back. Laisser faire, he said, "must never for a moment be allowed to stand in the way of the candid consideration of any promising proposal of social or industrial reform." It had done just that, and he, of all the classical economists, was the most scornful. Laisser faire is "totally destitute of all scientific authority" and has no place in economics, no more than communism has. That is so because economics, he said, and thousands have repeated, "pronounces no judgement on the worthiness or desirableness of the ends aimed at in such systems." Such judgments were more than wrong—they were harmful. "Decrees which are ordinarily given to the world in the name of Political Economy . . . in the main amount to a handsome ratification of the existing form of society as approximately perfect." [13]

His scientific detachment did not however prevent him from examining the idea, and its ethical assumptions particularly, more carefully than most others had done. Laisser faire, he said, assumes (a) that the interests of all men are harmonious, and (b) that all men understand and are able to advance their interests. He acknowledged that interests are in fact harmonious but only when they are "well understood." But, he said, it is not true that men understand their interests properly and are able to advance them. To suppose otherwise is to commit the "fatal" error of which the champions of laisser faire were forever guilty. Actually he did not accept the first assumption any more than the second. By declaring that interests are harmonious when well understood, he implied that only interests which are harmonious are genuine. That in turn implies that something other than interests (or other than "true" interests) is the cause of conflict. His explanation of these points was, it must be said, confusing. Nonetheless a summary statement of it is in order, because it has been repeated many times. It is indeed the model of most refutations of laisser faire.

Another feature of Cairne's lecture is the relationship he implied between policy and the positive side of economics. The latter, he said, established "natural laws." They are generalizations from the facts of economic be-

havior and they are unalterable in the same sense that
facts themselves are unalterable. To say the economy is
governed by natural law is then to say it is governed by
facts. Unfortunately, he continued, the statement has been
enlarged to mean the economy is not only governed by
facts but that the facts are good and that the economy is
therefore good. But for an economist to pass judgment on
them is wholly mistaken. The business of the economist is
to explain the facts, not to justify (or deplore) them. The
economist who champions noninterference (or its opposite) does not understand his job, Cairnes said.

Had Cairnes taken one more step he would have shown
that policy is related to science in the sense of being limited by the realities, that is, by the facts, of the economy.
(To have done so would have contradicted his assertion
that the positive and normative sides of economics are entirely separate; but one more inconsistency would not have
mattered.) Had Cairnes taken that step he would have
shown that a government, given the popular will, may do
only what the facts allow it to do. If he had said that, he
would have made explicit the principle on which the policy
of the century was based. As it was, he came very near
to saying it.

But then he said many other things as well, and they
clouded over what I believe was his intention. We know
that he denounced laisser faire, that he dismissed policy
altogether from scientific economics, that he then recalled
it in its factual aspect. In looking for a clear rule to guide
the economy, what was the public to make of all this?
Actually it did get some plain advice from him. After all
of his denunciation of laisser faire, he concluded that it
should be the "practical rule" of policy. What is singular
is that the advice was not given absent-mindedly, casually,
or without enthusiasm. On the contrary. He said that when
set against the principle of interference, and when interference is looked at in all of its implications, laisser faire is
"incomparably the safer guide." [14]

The men whose writing has been examined so far were
none of them consistent. Nor were others of the classical

school, not even Mill himself although he tried very hard to be. Of all of them, the most ruthless logician was Mill's father, but James was that way about a theory of government rather than about economic policy. Ricardo, who made more use of the analytical method than others, was not interested in the conceptual side of policy, although he was very attentive to the practice of it. Consistency was not an important element in the classical tradition. It was not disparaged in an overt way, and there certainly were many debates that turned on definition and deduction (like those over the labor theory of value and the theory of rent). But what seems to have mattered more in classical economics is that its ideas should be cogent and relevant than that they should be consistent.

The example of M'Culloch is informative. He is an amusing figure in the history of British economics because of his wooden consistency, his vast solemnity, his reverence for the ideas of Ricardo, and his proprietary manner with them. Taken all together, his qualities made him the archetype of the economist, and he is one of the few ever to be commemorated in a novel. It is *Crochet Castle* by Thomas Love Peacock, who as a member of the East India Office at the time of the Mills came to know them. Lady Clarinda says: "Well next to him sits Mr. MacQuedy, the Modern Athenian, who lays down the law about everything, and therefore may be taken to understand everything. He turns all the affairs of the world into questions of buying and selling. He is the Spirit of the Frozen Ocean to everything like romance and sentiment. He condenses their volume of steam into a drop of cold water in a moment. He has satisfied me that I am a commodity on the market, and that I ought to set myself at a high price." Still, when one compares him with the Rev. Dr. Folliott, a bluff, beefy clergyman whom Peacock wanted us to admire, MacQuedy does not come off badly at all. Right or wrong, he did respect ideas and didn't think that by using his mind he endangered his well-being or committed a social blunder.

One reason why the nineteenth century's ideas of policy

were inconsistent is that policy is a difficult subject. "The manner, occasion, and degree in which the State may interfere with the industrial freedom of its citizens is one of the most debatable and difficult questions of social science," Jevons said in 1882.[15] The question called for more knowledge and a more comprehensive view than positive economics did, and the economist who addressed himself to it needed a philosophic mind or at least would have found such a mind helpful. Not many had it in the century. Bentham did, but his influence was less than that of Ricardo, who did not. When the Ricardians wrote of policy, they necessarily had to consider political values and related issues. But either they did so in a rather superficial way, an instance being Senior's speculations about the power of government (described in the preceding chapter). Or more commonly they made what Mill called a flying excursion into the field of ethics and a swift return, instances of which are noticeable even today.

SPENCER AND THE PURE THEORY OF LAISSER FAIRE

It is helpful at this point to examine Herbert Spencer's ideas of economic policy. He usually is not thought of as an economist. Actually he was much more—a philosopher who tried to synthesize all knowledge. In his comprehensive scheme of things, economics was one element, and he knew it very well. In *The Man versus the State* he set forth his policy, which is significant for several reasons. It is more carefully reasoned than any of the writings of the recognized economists, including even the writing of Mill; it shows that consistency does not necessarily bring with it cogency, but in itself can be an alarming quality; and his policy shows what the liberalism of the classical economists was not.

What was most important to Spencer was the absence of restraint on the individual. That was the meaning he gave to freedom, and his policy was meant to provide freedom of that kind. It was a policy of pure laisser faire, or as pure as it ever is likely to be. Its singular feature was its being derived so closely from empirical psychology or

what he called "the science of life." Its content is the nature
of men, in their physical and, especially, in their psychological constitution. Both aspects of their nature are factual. Just as it is the nature of men to respond to their
environment physically, so it is their nature to respond psychologically. The responses show a regularity from which
generalizations can be made. The idea was not new, although Spencer's statement of it was. Smith had intimated
it in his remarks about natural behavior, like those in the
invisible hand passage above. He had gotten it from the
natural rights philosophers of the seventeenth century.
What all of them wanted to prove (or believe) was that
freedom is something which men must have and that to
deprive them of it is as unnatural as to deprive them of
their physical sustenance. None carried the idea as far
as Spencer did. He was a relentless logician, as they were
not; he was prepared to accept every implication, however preposterous, so long as it was deducible, but they
were not; and living in the age of Darwin, he called on
the authority of the new science of life (which in fact he
had anticipated) to support his findings about natural
rights. It proved their existence. He reasoned that to survive, an organism must have freedom of movement and
the power to do those things necessary for its survival.
Since the right to survival is indisputable, the right to
the means of survival must be also. To deprive an organism of freedom and power is to try to alter the fundamental conditions of its life (and of all life). Such an alter-
ation was indeed possible, he suggested, because by
changing the environment of an organism, its nature can
be changed. But the new being will be inferior to the old,
and hence changing it is an assault on the worth of nature. The great sin of legislators is to worsen the nature of
man by restricting his freedom.

There are two difficulties in Spencer's conception of freedom, and the reader probably has noticed them. The more
obvious is that unrestrained freedom is destructive. It is
destructive whether all men are equally capable of exercising it or whether they are not. Indeed, the more nearly

equal men are, the more protracted their conflict will be
—and the more destructive its outcome. Spencer acknowledged the difficulty and granted that some restraint is necessary when men act in groups. When they do, a distinction is made between the positive, or factual, character of
their rights, and their ethical character—the distinction
being between what they *can* do and what they *may* do.
He implied, however, that the distinction is something natural to men, citing the ways that primitive groups, without benefit of acknowledged law, impose restraints upon
behavior. In this way he tried to give the ethical distinction
a positive quality. The reasoning suggests that society
does not have to restrain individuals by law, that they
themselves can manage transgressions without the aid of a
coercive agency, the government. The second of the two
difficulties is the inclusion of power in the definition of freedom, so that freedom denotes the possession of means to
achieve an end as well as the absence of restraint on the
use of them. Spencer used freedom in this sense when he
said the individual not only has the right to survive but
also the right to the means of survival. Yet in examining
specific measures of policy, he used freedom to mean only
the absence of restraint—which was the meaning he gave
to it at the start of his book.

A legislator who went to Spencer for guidance would
come away with laisser faire in the purest form in which it
ever has been proposed. Consider Spencer's enumeration
of the laws that he believed restricted the liberty of the
individual. Some are what one would expect to find: factory legislation, the provision of direct relief, public ownership of utilities, the subsidizing of rail fares, and such.
But the list includes much more. Everything in it is, to be
sure, an instance of restraint. But the instances are so
unequally important that they could be brought together
only by a mind that was dedicated to the policy, a mind
that was meticulous and ruthlessly consistent. Included in
the list are the regulating of the sale of beer in Ireland and
Wales, the inspection of cattle in Scotland, the setting of
cab fares in London, the empowering of local boards

everywhere to set rates for the hire of horses, ponies, mules, and asses, a bill for the preservation of sea birds ("ensuring greater mortality of fish," he remarked with ambiguous humor), and so on—a wide net from which nothing escaped. Even the advocates of laisser faire must have had difficulty in getting exercised over every one of these restraints and they must have felt their case could have been strengthened by a shortening of the bill of particulars. Actually the bill had still more in it, and the addition suggests why Spencer's policy was not the received policy—why, in fact, he had little influence, although in the common interpretation his should have been the prevailing view of the century. His list of restraints included the laws that established free schools, compelled school attendance, made vaccination compulsory, and established public libraries. He did wish it known, he said, that in enumerating the ways in which the state deprived the individual of liberty, "no reflections are intended on the motives" of those who sponsored them.

He said the laws were wrong because they were enacted on the erroneous assumption that all social distress is remediable and that the state is responsible for remedying it. The assumption defied the facts of the science of life. "Reduced to its lowest terms, every proposal to interfere with citizens' activities further than by enforcing their mutual limitations, is a proposal to improve life by breaking through the fundamental conditions of life," he said. Liberalism, he contended, means limitation: "the liberty which a citizen enjoys is to be measured, not by the nature of the governmental machinery he lives under, whether representative or other, but by the relative paucity of the restraints it imposes on him." [16] All the state legitimately may do is to prevent the individual from invading the liberty of others. The state may coerce him negatively, but never positively. These ideas set Spencer quite apart from the classical economists. To them a measure of policy was liberal if it was consistent with the popular will. To him a measure was liberal if it was only negatively coercive. For a time Spencer was associated with *The*

Economist, and from it more than from any other source
the public obtained the idea that liberalism meant laisser
faire. But even *The Economist* never went so far as Spencer did.

An interesting byway in his intellectual history is the influence he had in Japan. His "synthetic philosophy," as
the doctrine in its entirety is called, is said to be closer to
Zen Buddhism than any other Western philosophy is. When
Japan was opened to the world, he was asked by some
Japanese leaders which Western institutions they would
be wise to adopt. As few as possible, he told them. There
have been even more notable examples of philosophers
being called upon to lay down the first principles of practical government. Locke wrote a constitution for the colony of Carolina, and John Adams later said it showed how
mistaken even the greatest minds could be about the practice of government. Rousseau wrote a constitution for
Corsica, and it was another bad piece of work, although
no more reactionary than *The Social Contract,* of which it
was a careful application. In the application of economic
ideas, there is a curious episode involving Smith. He is
known to have worked in the study of the Chancellor of
the Exchequer in London when the budget of 1767 was
prepared and he may have had a hand in it. It provoked
massive opposition from the merchants in the American
colonies and revived the nonimportation agreements that
were a step on the way to the Revolution. Actually, the
budget reduced some levies on the colonies, but it was ac-
companied by the Townshend Acts, which provided for
its strict enforcement. Among the philosophers and economists who spoke to kings, Spencer was unique. He did not
prescribe a course for the Japanese; he proscribed one.
Consistent with his doctrine, he was negatively coercive.[17]

5 *The Theory of Policy in Mill*

We come at last to John Stuart Mill. To include still other
economists would not alter the point of this chapter or
make it any more plain. The point is this: Liberal economic

policy authorizes the state to do whatever the people want it to do and it is able to do. For additional evidence that liberalism is not synonymous with laisser faire the reader can consult the informative book of D. H. MacGregor, *Economic Thought and Policy*. However, that book so emphasizes the opposition to free markets and makes so little of the support for them that the reader is liable to conclude the economists of the nineteenth-century were in favor of the state's directing the economy. Such a conclusion is quite mistaken. The economists favored neither extreme. How far they wished the state to go toward either was the leading question in their theory of policy.

Mill tried to answer that question. Other writers, he said, had considered only a few measures of policy, such as the Poor Laws or the Factory Acts, and had pretty much neglected the others. Nevertheless they had stated their opinions in the form of very general arguments that were meant to apply to other measures as well. Those arguments revealed a strong bias for either laisser faire or for its opposite. But the writers did not say how far either principle was to be carried nor did they seem to be clear in their own minds on the point. Mill hoped, in the *Principles*, to provide some help in deciding the limits of laisser faire.

THE OBJECTIONS TO INTERFERENCE

He distinguished two kinds of interference by the government in the economy: authoritative and nonauthoritative. The former is prescriptive or coercive while the latter is suggestive or optional. The government may form a bank and give it a monopoly of all banking transactions. That interference would be authoritative. Or it may operate a bank in competition with banks that are privately owned. That would be nonauthoritative. Of the two forms, authoritative interference presents the greater danger to liberty. Interference of this kind should be more limited in its application and needs a greater necessity to justify it. From some areas, it should be excluded altogether. In a sentence that suggests the great passages in the essay *On Liberty* that he was to write ten years later, Mill said, "there is

a circle around every individual human being, which no
government, be it that of one, of a few, or of the many,
ought to be permitted to overstep." [18] The question is just
what the circle encompasses. It includes, Mill answered,
the thoughts and feelings of the individual, the part of his
behavior that affects only him, the part that does no injury to others, and the part that affects others only by example. That interference could invade these areas was
the first objection to it.

What Mill here insisted on was similar to what the liberals of the seventeenth and eighteenth century meant by
the inviolability of natural rights. It was the meaning also
of his second objection to authoritative interference. The
objection was that each additional responsibility assigned
to government added to the total of its powers and hence
to the danger of their being used to deprive the individual
of his liberty. He warned against thinking that a democratic government (as he defined it) could be trusted
with powers that would be dangerous in a dictatorial government. Indeed there was, he said, even more need to limit
the powers of democratic government, because it is ruled
by public opinion, and from public opinion there is no ap-
peal. Another objection to authoritative interference is that
it adds to the total work of government and reduces the
efficiency with which any one part is done. The objection
was utilitarian, and he meant that most business is done
best by the people whose business it is. His final objection—and "one of the strongest"—is that authoritative interference does for the people what they, for the sake of cultivating their "active faculties," should do for themselves.
The greater is the authority of the government, Mill said,
the greater is the number of able people who are a part of
it. The smaller then is the number outside government
who are able to protect the people from it. All of these objections created a strong case against authoritative interference. They led to the conclusion that: "*Laisser-faire*,
in short, should be the general practise: every departure
from it, unless required by some great good, is a certain
evil." [19]

What counted most with Mill were the utilitarian objections. His case for laisser faire is summarized in his statement that the government does not know so well as the people what they want and cannot provide it so well as they can provide it for themselves. Yet when the case is put this way—with the assumptions clearly implied—it invites some questions: Is it a fact that the people always know better than the government what is good for them? Supposing it is a fact, can one say they always can do more for themselves than the government can do for them? And supposing all this to be true, can we be sure that an individual acting freely, in his own interest, will not injure other individuals? Mill met these questions explicitly, and answered—No, these are not always facts. He acknowledged there was a case for intervention, and most of his explanation of the principles of policy is about that case. What he had to say *against* laisser faire is more interesting and longer than what he said *for* it.

Individuals do not always know their own interest as consumers, Mill stated, and they are particularly unknowing about those objects of expenditure that "raise the character of human beings." They are the objects that are the most important in the doctrine of utilitarianism. Mill made education an example. Individuals will not all of them spend enough on it if they may themselves decide what the amount shall be. Some will, but those who need education most will spend the least. "The uncultivated cannot be competent judges of cultivation," he said. He said also that government without being presumptuous could assume that it was more cultivated than the mass of people. It therefore should provide schools, although it should not prohibit people from providing schools for themselves. Also, it should compel parents to send their children to an elementary school of some kind. The interference would be nonauthoritative in providing schools and authoritative in compelling attendance. Mill justified both kinds of interference by stating that the failure of parents to educate their children was an injury to the children and, because of the effects of ignorance, to everyone else in society as

well. That circle drawn around every person within which
his rights were private and supreme did not include parental authority in all of its forms. When Mill excepted education from the rule of laisser faire, he was therefore consistent with the premises of his policy.

Something more should be said about his views on education and other forms of consumption. He did not believe that every one of the wants of the individual was beyond the judgment of the economist. Those which were
beyond it were placed there by an ethical decision of the
economist. He ignored them because he wished to, not because he felt incompetent and hence had to. Mill did not
believe it impossible to compare the wants of different
individuals or to draw a conclusion about how much a
given quantity of consumption satisfied each person. He
would have been puzzled and then saddened by the
Olympian attitude that today's economists take toward
consumer wants. (But he would have tried very hard to
understand it, believing as he did that he could learn
something from everyone.) Ruskin said that Mill's great
mistake was that he passed too little judgment on the
quality of consumption and production. An economist today would say that Mill made far too many judgments.

Mill's disposition to make such judgments is an aspect of
his ideas and behavior that is not much commented on. It
does not square well with his insisting upon tolerance.
But it can hardly be missed. It was, it seems to me, a mixture of several things. First, there was his utilitarianism,
within which the judging of ends was perfectly in order.
One cannot decide what is the greatest good of the greatest number without having first decided what the good is.
It could be simply what the greatest number want it to
be. But more often it is what men of discernment, like Mill
himself, believe it ought to be. There was also in his thinking an element of the Whig conception of freedom. In that
view, not all persons were equally capable of freedom,
and those who were had an obligation to improve those
who were not. When Mill was a young man, some prominent
people, mostly Whigs, formed the Edinburgh Society for

the Diffusion of Useful Knowledge among the lower classes.
James Mill was a member, and the chairman was Lord
Brougham, a leading Whig and a contributor of economic
articles to *The Edinburgh Review*. Peacock called it "The
Steam Intellect Society" and scored off Brougham in the
same novel in which he made fun of M'Culloch. There
was still another element in the mixture and the one
that is the least pleasing to an admirer of Mill. He was
given not only to forming opinions about the behavior of
others but of being censorious, to want not only to improve their characters but to meddle and fuss with them,
to be at times the maiden aunt or bluenose, or (more
charitably) Cato the Censor. This element will surprise
those who know Mill only as the champion of individual
liberty. But a fair reading of his *Principles* cannot fail
to disclose this element. It may be thought not to count for
much, especially when set against his declarations for tolerance and privacy. Indeed in his chapter on the future of
the working class, Mill rebuked those who would treat the
poor as if they were children, who would think for them
instead of encouraging them to think for themselves. Yet in
telling the poor some of the things that were good for
them, Mill was doing just what he advised others not to
do. He may have been helpful in doing this but that is not
necessarily a justification for it. Mill was inconsistent to assert both that men are their own masters and that some
of them should not follow their inclinations.

He probably would have resolved the dilemma by saying that if the poor are helped now, they in time will become capable of making the proper choices. But the very
idea of "proper" is inconsistent with liberalism of the classical and nonutilitarian kind. What counts is whether or
not everyone is free to make choices in as rational a manner as he is capable of, together with the corollary that if a
choice made by one person will affect another it must have
the other's consent. The act of choice is important, not the
thing chosen. Mill did not entirely accept this idea, but he
was even farther from rejecting it. His equivocation allowed the officious element to enter his doctrine. To over-

look that element is to ignore something that helps to explain a major inconsistency in his economic policy. The inconsistency was to state that what is most important to the individual—as his character undoubtedly is—should be farthest from the power of the state, and then to propose ways in which the state could improve his character. To be sure, Mill tried to remove the inconsistency by saying that the failure of a man to develop his character can be injurious to others. Yet if that is so, even character loses its position as an end and becomes a means to something else (the improvement of the character of others?). Moreover, what meaning is left in the declaration that there should be "some space in human existence . . . sacred from authoritative intrusion"? As Ernest Barker said, the liberal view is that the improvement of a man's character is the business of no one but himself.

THE EXCEPTIONS TO LAISSER FAIRE

Mill believed the government should restrict more than consumption. He also believed it should place some restrictions on what individuals could do in labor markets, in the conduct of business, and in the making of contracts. His reason was that individuals do not always know what their interest is; that when they do know it, they may not be able to promote it; and that even when they do know their interest and are able to promote it, the interest of some may not be in harmony with the interest of others. On these considerations he based five exceptions to laisser faire, and they were considerably more important than the exception he took to complete freedom of consumption. They were of more practical consequence, more interesting from the viewpoint of the theory of policy, and more instructive about the duties of the government and the governed. They also show the difference between Mill's method and that of other economists. Where they examined a few outstanding issues of policy and made some swift generalizations, he began with the principle of laisser faire, considered whether or not it should govern all economic conduct, found numerous instances in which it should not, and then generalized about the exceptions. What he said is most clear if we know the point from which he began. It was that "most persons take a juster and more intelligent view of their own interest, and of the means of promoting it" than the government can take. However, there are "some large and very conspicuous exceptions." [20]

First, people do not always know their interest. Incapacity and immaturity prevent some from knowing it, and others act for them. The question, then, is how much power the others should be permitted to have. An example is the interest of a child. Mill's view was that the interest of children could be cared for much better by government than by their parents. He expressed the view forcefully and in language much different from the well-tempered prose for which he is celebrated. He wrote of the "constant abuse" of parental power, of "domestic tyrants," of children being "brutally ill-treated" and even murdered by their parents, of "the metaphysical scruples" that prevented government from interfering directly with the family, and of other matters that disclose the censorious element in his thinking. (When Mill wrote about the family in any of its aspects, from the authority of husbands and fathers to the number of children, he often was intemperate.) The point of this exception to laisser faire is that it justified child labor laws, which the Factory Acts originally were. In Mill's day they had begun to control the work of women. Such control was a mistaken application of the exception, he said. Women would be able to take care of themselves very well if the laws were repealed that gave husbands a monopoly of family property, granted them coercive power, permitted moral and physical tyranny, etc.

Second, an individual cannot know just what his interest will be in the distant future. The reason is not incapacity or immaturity but simply the impossibility of perfectly accurate prediction. The point has an important bearing on the freedom of individuals to make contracts.

That freedom always is presumed to be an essential feature of liberalism. But in exercising it an individual may impose obligations on himself that in the future will abridge his freedom. This can happen because he cannot know at the time a contract is made whether or not the terms later will become burdensome. Mill did not go so far as to repudiate the principle of leaving contracts free. But he did say the principle should be applied sparingly to contracts in perpetuity. The law, he said, should refuse to enforce them if they impose conditions about which a contracting party cannot have formed a reasonable judgment at the time the contract was made. In other words, an individual should be allowed to break the contract. If however he is not allowed to break it on his own choosing, he should be allowed to do so upon making out a sufficient case before an impartial body.

Third, the interest of one individual may conflict with that of others. If it does, the state should limit the freedom of the few for the sake of the many. From this point Mill developed some quite large economic powers of government, such as the control of corporation directors, the public ownership of enterprise, the fixing of monopoly prices, and the confiscating of monopoly profits. His reasoning is curious. Starting with the idea that individuals *know* their interest better than government can, he concluded the government should not interfere with the management of private affairs except when it should. It should, he said, when otherwise the affairs of one group would be managed for it by another. The point is similar, perhaps identical, with his first exception to laisser faire. But here he gave the example of the directors of a joint-stock company using their position to the detriment of shareholders other than themselves. Whatever can be said about the inefficiency or dishonesty of government, Mill wrote, can be said with equal force about the behavior of corporate directors. He did not, however, want their work to be taken over by government officials. All of the practical and most of the ethical arguments for laisser faire made him oppose such a solution. It is an odd solution in any event: It was that the government should operate, not merely regulate, a private enterprise, but should not own it.

He mentioned the solution in his remarks about the responsibility of government for the proper conduct of private enterprise. He believed government had that responsibility and he applied the idea to many more things than the supervision of corporate directors. He believed government was responsible for the conduct of monopolies; otherwise they could use their price power to tax the public. Local governments should own some, he said, like gas and waterworks. Others, like canals and railroads, should be regulated. One method of regulation that he proposed was the familiar one of the government's setting their rates. He also proposed the novel method of permitting the monopolies to use their price power for a limited period after which the government would confiscate and operate them. The implied theory was that the monopoly profits over the allotted time would equal the capital value of the enterprise if its prices were competitive. At the end of the period, the public would acquire ownership of the enterprise it had bought by paying higher than competitive prices for the service. All of this is substantial intervention. But Mill had one more proposal about the monopoly problem. It was that the government in certain circumstances should establish an enterprise and while retaining ownership, give it over to a private company to operate. The proposal was just the opposite of that noted above— and almost as odd. That above was government operation of private enterprise; this was private operation of government enterprise.

In explaining the third exception, Mill continually shifted the argument and made it encompass more and more intervention. He seemed to be asking the reader a series of questions to which the answer always was supposed to be Yes. Is it not true that, if as a shareholder you name a director to manage the business you both own, he may be in a position to increase his income at your expense? If this is granted, does it not follow that we have an in-

stance of self-interest producing disharmony instead of
the harmony that laisser faire presupposes? Is it not true
that the disharmony would be as great as that produced
by government, even a government that is inefficient and
corrupt? Does it not follow that government management
of a corporation's affairs would be no worse than private
management? Have we not then established a justification
for government intervention in order to remove disharmony? (The reader's "Yes" would be fairly weak at this
point.) If the government may intervene in corporate affairs, may it not also intervene in other instances in which
there is disharmony? Is not monopoly such an instance?
And are there not a number of ways to solve the monopoly
problem? Is not government ownership one way, as well as
government operation, government regulation, government
confiscation of profits? . . . What began as a modest observation about corporate affairs ended in a stunning collection
of proposals for intervention.

Fourth, an individual acting alone may be unable to
promote his own interest, even though he knows it very
well, even though he is acting for himself, and even
though what he wants is in harmony with what others
want. The reason is that he can get it only if all of the
others also act to get it. Mill gave two examples. One
was the reduction of working hours without a reduction
of daily wages. If all workers wanted this reduction but
tried individually to get it, all would fail. If one tried to
work ten hours when the working day was twelve, he
would lose his job or be paid less than the others. If all
agreed to work ten hours but had no way to enforce the
agreement, it would break down. Anyone who wanted
higher wages could earn them by working twelve hours
while the others were working ten. If higher wages rather
than shorter hours were what most of the workers really
wanted, in time everyone again would be working twelve
hours—but at the old hourly wage. To be effective, the
agreement would have to be enacted into law.

The other example was the Wakefield system of colonization. It was a piece of ingenuity of the kind that al-

ways has fascinated economists. Usually the device contrives to redirect self-interest in an artful way in order to promote a public good. An earlier instance was the mercantilist plan to increase the population by subsidizing marriages and taxing bachelors, the tax to finance the subsidy. (Reversing the plan is a possible remedy for overpopulation.) Another was Ricardo's optimum tariff on grain: an amount equal to the additional tax burden on agriculture, the result being a proper allocation of capital between it and industry. Still another is the proposal made in this century to fix exchange rates, auction off import licenses, and subsidize exports. Wakefield proposed that the colonial government put a high price on land and use the proceeds to pay the transportation costs of immigrants. The effects would be: (a) to keep the immigrants employed at nonagricultural work until they had enough to buy land, thereby providing a supply of labor for the building of roads, canals, and urban industry; (b) preventing the immigrants from acquiring more land than they could cultivate efficiently; (c) populating the colony while relieving the old countries of crowding. Today, in the economics of development, the plan would be described as a method of securing in an underpopulated country the optimum rates of growth in agriculture, in urban industries, and of investment yielding external economics.

There are significant implications in the examples that Mill used to illustrate his fourth exception. The first example showed the inability of an individual worker to change wages in a competitive market. What it proved was that competition can be restricted only by concerted action that has the support of law. To use the same example to illustrate the inadequacy of self-interest is to imply that competition among producers does not always serve their interest. That is not a novel idea. What is novel is to find it in the last great work of classical economics. One reasonably can ask why the interest of the workers should be placed before that of the rest of the population. One can argue that the workers' interest should come first, but Mill did not argue this way (except if one wishes to infer

the argument from his very general proposition, made near
the beginning of the *Principles,* that while the forces regulating production cannot be changed, those regulating
distribution can be; I believe the inference is not justifiable). He simply implied that if something is to the advantage of the workers, they should be assisted in obtaining it—and a predisposition toward the working class is
not something usually ascribed to classical economics. All
that Mill was careful to say was that the restricting of
hours and the raising of hourly wages *might* cause unemployment and hence not be to the workers' advantage.
Whether or not any particular instance of regulation
would be to the worker's advantage was, Mill said, always "a question of fact." Here one ought to recall the
similarity of Mill's position to that of Senior.

The example of colonization also illustrated another
failing of a competitive market and one of a much different
kind. It showed that the total returns from a particular economic act, such as an investment in roads, do not all of
them go to the person who makes the investment and that
what he does not receive other people do. The marginal
private return is less than the marginal social return, it
would be said in welfare economics. In a free market, if
the (marginal) private cost of investment is greater than the
private return, even though less than the social return, the
investment will not be made. The economy nevertheless
would benefit if it were made, because total output would
increase. Government, in Mill's scheme of things, would
contrive to have the investment made.

Fifth, some persons are not permitted to act for themselves, and others must act for them. The reason here is not
immaturity, as it is with children, nor that the person voluntarily authorizes someone else to act for him, as a
shareholder does. It is that custom or necessity—or both—
does not allow a person to act for himself. For example, a
person who seeks charity is not allowed to specify the
amount or anything else about it. These decisions are made
by those who dispense it. The question then is whether the
givers alone should determine how charity is to be granted

or whether government should specify the procedure. Mill answered in favor of government. It can, he said, make the provision of relief what it should be: absolutely certain to persons in need and the granting of it impersonal, fair, predictable, and respectful of the privacy of the recipient. "The dispensers of public relief have no business to be inquisitors." That is the tolerant Mill, not the censorious.

In explaining this exception to laisser faire, he stated his view of the Poor Laws. It was that the recipient never should be made as well off as those who supported themselves. The reason was not justice. He did not, for example, argue that those who worked for their living deserved more than those who did not. Nor did he in any other way relate his view to the ethical aspect of the labor theory of value, which was that income earned by labor was ethically superior to that which was not. Mill's reason was a practical one and exemplified his utilitarianism. It was that relief should be given in such a way as to prompt those who received it to greater exertion and independence so that as soon as possible they could do without it. The idea was derived from a psychological conjecture that runs through the history of economics (and was especially important to the mercantilists)—namely, that in adversity begins industry. Mill carried it a little further and said that adversity must not be so great as to leave people hopeless nor so slight as to make them indolent. There is, it seems, an optimum amount. What he believed were the causes of poverty, hence of the need for relief, also is interesting. They were, he said, the excessively unequal distribution of wealth in his day and the fact that the habits of the people were neither "temperate" nor "prudent" (Cato again). He did not attribute poverty to the structural and cyclical unemployment of his time.

The fifth exception to laisser faire meant the government should control the conduct of people who act for others. Mill applied it to colonies, as well as to poor relief, and the clear implication was that government should direct colonial development instead of allowing it to be determined by individuals acting in their interest as they

understand it. A colonist should not be allowed to make
an investment that is profitable to him if it retards the
development of the colony. In making a long-term investment, he is acting in the interest of others, not only of himself, even though he may be indifferent to the fact. Future generations will be affected by what he does now.
Mill said that acts which have consequences extending
indefinitely beyond the persons making them, "to the interests of the nation or of posterity," are acts "for which
society in its collective capacity is alone able, and alone
bound, to provide." He could also have argued—as he did
in making his second exception to laisser faire—that such
acts have the consequences of a long-term contract, because future generations are bound by investment decisions over which they can have no control. After laying
down the very broad principle of collective responsibility for the welfare of posterity, the specific application
Mill made of it was so modest as to be anticlimactic.
The application was the Wakefield system again. Nevertheless, Mill was aware that the principle could be used in
many other ways. Indeed it could be used in ways he did
not acknowledge. I can think of no reason why it should
apply only to investment in colonies. If it is wrong for a
colonist to ignore the interests of the future, it also is
wrong for an individual in the mother country to do so. If
a colonial government may control investment, so may a
home government; and that requires control of consumption also. Mill's idea is a variation on an idea in the theory
of growth, namely that a market economy underestimates
the value of long-term investment and hence grows less
rapidly than an economy in which government controls investment; the government is more effective because it takes
a longer view than individuals take. If true, this means that
long-term investment made by the market adds less to the
income of the near future than it takes from the income of
the far future, and it is analogous to the proposition in welfare economics than in some market transactions at any moment of time the gains to those making it are less than the
costs imposed on those outside it. Mill could have applied

his fifth exception to such instances. He did in fact apply the fourth to them.

THE ARGUMENT FOR UNLIMITED INTERFERENCE

The use to which he did put the fifth exception was something different. Inasmuch as individuals should not be allowed to act in a way that damages the future, they should be encouraged to act in a way that assists it. If they will not do so voluntarily, the government is justified in acting in their place. He therefore came to the conclusion that government was justified (if not obliged) to do anything which was desirable for the future but was not profitable for individuals to undertake in the present. From that Mill went on to say that government also should do anything which was desirable for the present but which individuals in the present did not find it profitable to undertake. The extension of the idea brought him around to Smith's proposition that government should engage in works of great usefulness that private enterprise would neglect if they were unprofitable. The conclusion is that government may do anything which is to the interest of the present and the future to have done. Lest that be thought an overstatement, the reader shall have it in Mill's words:

It may be said generally, that anything which it is desirable should be done for the general interest of mankind or of future generations, or for the present interests of those members of the community who require external aid, but which is not of a nature to remunerate individuals or associations for undertaking it, is in itself a suitable thing to be undertaken by government: though, before making the work their own, governments ought always to consider if there be any rational probability of its being done on what is called the voluntary principle, and if so, whether it is likely to be done in a better or more effectual manner by government agency than by the zeal and liberality of individuals.[21]

The qualification about voluntary action, it should be noted, is itself qualified: government should allow philanthropies to undertake unprofitable but useful work only if they can do it more effectively than government can. That is not consistent with Mill's view that by acting for themselves individuals become more effective.

At this point a disciple of laisser faire must be troubled over what was made of it by one who is renowned as its great expositor. But there is still more. After concluding his statement of the five exceptions to laisser faire, Mill warned against using them in a way that would prevent government intervention when it otherwise seemed necessary. He wished it known that if intervention seemed to be called for and could not be justified by one of the five exceptions, government should intervene nevertheless. He said: "In the particular circumstances of a given age or nation, there is scarcely anything, really important to the general interest, which it may not be desirable, or even necessary, that the government should take upon itself, not because private individuals cannot effectually perform it, but because they will not." [22] They most likely will not in those places where the rulers are superior in ability and purpose to the ruled, as in a country conquered by a people who are more energetic and cultivated than the natives are. Mill's remarks at this point would be coldly received by the underdeveloped countries today, but most of them would welcome his rejection of the market as the guide to development. Mill, to be sure, did say that what government does it should do in a way that prepares people to do in time the same thing for themselves. But that time can be very far into the future, and meanwhile government direction may do more to make people dependent on it than to teach them how to do without it. Not unfairly, one may recall Mill to himself. The last sentence quoted above is on the last page of the *Principles*. On the last page of *On Liberty*, he said that a state which tried to do everything for the people would find it really could not do very much, because the people in time would not be worth doing much for.

THE AMBIGUITY IN MILL

The ambiguity in Mill is formidable. Among the things that are not clear is what he meant by freedom. As a utilitarian he believed in freedom as a means and not as something that was always worthwhile in itself. He believed men should be free because only by being so could they reach their goals. But if one supposes they may reach their goals without being free, does that mean freedom has no value? One cannot be sure. At other times he wrote that freedom was an end in itself, and then he was not a utilitarian. Another uncertain point is whether freedom, as either a means or an end, meant the absence of restraint or the possession of power. When he made it a means, one is not clear in what order he ranked the purposes it was meant to serve. The ambiguity on these points becomes most noticeable when one brings together all of the arguments for and against laisser faire and examines their relations to each other. Of the four in favor of laisser faire, the first two imply that freedom is an end; but the last two imply it is a means. All of the arguments against laisser faire imply either that freedom is not an effective means to the ends to which it is directed or that the ends are not desirable. Some imply that freedom means the possession of power (the first, second, and fourth exceptions), while the others imply it can be either that or the absence of restraint. When Mill stated the ends that either freedom or intervention was meant to serve, he sometimes made them, abstractly, the moral or mental energies of the individual; sometimes, specifically, qualities like diligence, enterprise, or self-reliance; sometimes, impersonal and abstract, like the efficiency of government or of the economy, or impersonal and specific like the production of particular commodities and services. It is plausible to think he placed the qualities of individuals above the other ends, but that is not prescriptive enough to tell legislators how to make policy or the public how to judge it.

These detailed comments may seem to the reader to be of questionable value. My reason for making them comes from believing that most of what has been written about Mill is too brief or too particular. Some of the histories of economic thought contain a very fair summary of Mill's arguments for and against laisser faire. But by omitting the details, they give his theory of policy an appearance of completeness and consistency that it really does not have. Particular studies of the theory emphasize one or another aspect to the exclusion of the rest. Robbins shows that Mill was not doctrinaire about laisser faire and that he was sympathetic to socialism. But Mill's theory of policy was much more than that. MacGregor emphasizes Mill's opposition to laisser faire, citing among other things his denunciation of the idea in a letter to Carlyle in 1833 (a letter which in my opinion has been rather overworked) and in a speech in the House of Commons in 1868. One would suppose that Mill meant nothing at all when he wrote that "laisser faire, in short, should be the general practise." The statement is certainly difficult to interpret but not so difficult as to justify its being discarded as meaningless.

There are those who have supposed Mill was in favor of nothing but laisser faire. Most have been of an earlier age, when denouncing laisser faire was not so easy as it has become in the twentieth century. Among them have been the leading American lawyers of the nineteenth century. Benjamin R. Twiss writes about them in his book on the Constitution and laisser faire. He reports that in 1909 Roscoe Pound said that every liberally educated lawyer in America from 1850 onward was required to read in Mill's *Principles* the chapter entitled "Of the Grounds and Limits of the Laisser-Faire or Non-Interference Principle." This is the chapter on which most of my comments are based. Pound said that American lawyers got their extreme view of liberty of contract from Mill. It was a view that carried free exchange as far as possible and then a little farther. Twiss cites the argument, made by railroad lawyers in a rate-fixing case, that to fix prices is to deprive the seller of his property.[23] We may recall that in his third exception to laisser faire, Mill proposed that the government set prices in a market where they otherwise would be set by a monopoly. One wonders just what it was that the law students read—an expurgated edition of the *Principles* or those passages they expected to be quizzed on by teachers predisposed to laisser faire.

THE GENERAL CONSCIENCE AS THE GUIDE TO POLICY

The ambiguity in Mill's theory of policy is not the point at which one cares to end a commentary on him. One would like to find some idea that helps to bring together the parts of the theory, that dispels at least some of their ambiguity, and that relates the premise of his theory to that of the other liberal economists of the century. I do not know of any idea that does all of this, although it may be somewhere in his writings. However, some help is provided by a remark Mill made about "the general conscience," by which he seems to have meant the ethical values which all "persons of ordinary good intentions either believe already, or can be induced to believe." [24] The general conscience, he said, was the justification for prohibitory regulations—those forms of authoritative interference that restrict the behavior of individuals. He did not say it justified prescriptive measures—those forms that require individuals to do certain things. But most measures of policy can be stated in either way. Certainly all that Mill proposed can be. What all of them had in common was, I suggest, that they recommended themselves to a man of ordinary good intentions. Or they could be made to do so. Such a man would or should believe that individuals can look after themselves better than government can look after them. Hence, laisser faire would recommend itself to him as a general rule. But he would take exception to it when it produced results not to his liking: poor education, child labor, monopoly prices, long hours of work, and any other of the problems that Mill's proposals were meant to solve.

The general conscience helps us to understand the principle by which Mill marked off the areas of the economy he believed should be controlled by government and those he believed should not be. It relates the different forms

of control to each other by showing what all of them
have in common. It also shows why Mill refused to be
bound by the principles of economic policy that he himself laid down—why, that is, after carefully explaining the
circumstances in which exceptions could be taken to
laisser faire he appended an omnibus exception by which
control of almost any kind could be justified. That last exception had only one limit—the general conscience. Finally,
the idea of the general conscience implies there is no inconsistency in a policy that calls for both intervention and
nonintervention or both controlled and uncontrolled markets. The idea does that by implying intervention can
increase the freedom of some individuals by adding to
their power and can protect others against a loss of freedom by removing conflicts of interest.

The ultimate principle on which Mill based his economic policy, was, I submit, that government may do
anything which men of good intentions believe it should
do *or can be made to believe it should do*. His principle
was similar to but not identical with that of the liberal
economists of the century who were not utilitarians. It was
similar in that Mill and the others believed government
may do whatever the people want it to do and it is able
to do. Mill differed from them in believing that the wants
of the people should not be taken as given. He did not believe, as the others did, that government must be limited
by what clearly could be established as the opinion of the
people. Mill believed the formation of opinion was itself
one of the responsibilities of government. It must be so, because in his view government was responsible for improving the people, for strengthening their character, elevating
their desires, and enlarging their views. This is the difference that separated the liberals who were utilitarian from
those who were not. It is suggested by Mill's distinction
between what people "either already believe" and what
they "can be induced to believe."

The distinction, made so casually and quickly, is enor-
mously important. The utilitarian view allows for much
more government intervention than the nonutilitarian (or

traditional) view of liberalism. That is so because what people can be induced to believe is almost always more than what they do believe. It also is so because government itself is to the utilitarians an agency that forms beliefs. There are ways (like the market and the polls) of knowing what people *do* believe and what the general conscience *is*, even though the ways often are rough and ready. The traditional liberal therefore can specify in a practical way just what is the limit to government power. There is no way of knowing what the general conscience *ought* to be, because in a liberal society there are no absolutes by which conscience is formed. Those governments that do claim to know what the general conscience ought to be are none of them liberal in either the traditional or utilitarian sense. They are in fact based on some form of political idealism, such as communism or fascism. The utilitarians, to be sure, do propose the rule that government may do only those things that improve the people, but the rule merely restates the problem, because it does not explain what those things are and what improvement is.

AFTER MILL

Both the traditional and the utilitarian views of liberalism help to explain the measures of economic policy enacted by government in the nineteenth century. In time the utilitarian view enlarged its influence, not to displace traditional liberalism but to compete with and to challenge it. In the twentieth century, governments have been guided more by what they believe the people ought to want and less by what the people clearly do want. My evidence for this is the increase in those measures of economic policy that are controversial, difficult to enforce, divisive, and subject to continual change. In the transition—in both its factual and doctrinal aspects—is the answer to one of the great questions of our day: How did liberalism change from an economic policy of limitation to one of comprehensive control? The answer, put very simply, is that traditional liberalism was replaced by utilitarian liberalism. Those who today propose comprehensive planning in the name of liberalism are utilizing the opportunities that utilitarianism supplies. Those who adhere to the traditional view of liberalism are often pained that the advocates of planning also call themselves liberals. To do so is, in the traditional view, a travesty on the word liberal. But it really is not, because in the nineteenth century liberalism by admitting utilitarian ideas became ambiguous. And the ambiguity explains something more important than the confusion of names. It explains why traditional liberals believe that what the planning liberals propose to do will in the end produce a dictatorial state, and it explains why the latter dismiss the belief. Ironically, about the only figure of the past whom both admire is Mill.

Mill did not begin the transition from traditional liberalism. Utilitarianism is much older. Bentham was a force, and he in turn was influenced by Hume and others. But Mill made the first comprehensive effort to state the utilitarian theory of liberalism. Those who followed enlarged either on his principles of economic policy or on those of the traditional liberals. It is with Mill, therefore, that these studies are concluded.

NOTES

1 THE CLASSICAL PSYCHOLOGY OF LIBERALISM

1 Adam Smith, *The Theory of Moral Sentiments* (London, 1892), pp. 119, 264-265, 332.
2 *Ibid.*, p. 264.
3 Adam Smith, "The Principles which lead and direct Philosophical Enquiries; illustrated by the History of Ancient Physics," *Essays on Philosophical Subjects* (London, 1795), p. 106.
4 Smith *Essays*, p. 143.
5 Adam Smith, *Lectures on Justice, Police, Revenue and Arms*, ed. Edwin Cannan (Oxford, 1896), p. 205.
6 Cicero *De officiis*, trans. C. W. Keyes, i, 7.
7 Adam Smith, *The Wealth of Nations*, ed. Edwin Cannan (New York, 1937), pp. 683, 794.
8 *Ibid.*, pp. 59-60, 128-129, 460.
9 See F. H. Knight, "The Sickness of Liberal Society," *Freedom and Reform* (New York, 1947), p. 377.

2 THE POLITICS OF THE CLASSICAL ECONOMISTS

1 David Hume, "Of the First Principles of Government," and "Of the Original Contract," *Essays Moral, Political, and Literary* in *Philosophical Works*, III (Edinburgh, 1826).
2 Adam Smith, *Lectures on Justice, Police, Revenue and Arms*, ed. Edwin Cannan (Oxford, 1896), pp. 11-13; and

The Wealth of Nations, ed. Edwin Cannan (New York, 1937), pp. 670, 674.

3   Hume, "Of the Rise and Progress of the Arts and Sciences," *op. cit.,* III, 126; and "Of Commerce," *ibid.,* III, 301.

4   Hume, "That Politics May Be Reduced to a Science," *op. cit.,* III, 24-25; "Of the First Principles of Government," *ibid.,* III, 32; "Of the Origin of Government," *ibid.,* III, 38-39; and "Of the Dignity or Meanness of Human Nature," *ibid.,* III.

5   "Of the First Principles of Government," *op. cit.,* III.

6   John Locke, *Of Civil Government, Two Treatises* (London, 1940), p. 180.

7   Adam Smith, *The Theory of Moral Sentiments* (London, 1892), p. 219.

8   John Rae, *Life of Adam Smith* (London, 1895), p. 149.

9   Smith, *Lectures,* p. 69. Hume, "Of Passive Obedience," *op. cit.,* III.

10 "Of Commerce," *op. cit.,* III, 298.

11 *The Wealth of Nations,* pp. 79, 66-67, 391.

12 David Ricardo, *Principles of Political Economy and Taxation* (London, 1911), p. 61.

13 *Ibid.,* pp. 61-62.

14 Edwin Cannan, "Ricardo in Parliament," *Economic Journal* IV (1894), 415-417.

15 J. R. M'Culloch, *Principles of Political Economy* (Edinburgh, 1843), p. 16.

16 *Lectures,* p. 14.

17 See below, pp. 66-67.

18 James Mill, *An Essay on Government* (Cambridge, 1937) ch. viii.
    John Stuart Mill, *Considerations on Representative Government* (London, 1861), p. 175.

19 The review appeared originally in the *Edinburgh Review* in 1845 and was reprinted in Senior's *Historical and Philosophical Essays* (London, 1865), I.

20 M'Culloch, *op. cit.,* p. 57.

21 *The Wealth of Nations,* p. 460.

22 Matthew Arnold, "The Function of Criticism at the Present Time," *Essays in Criticism* [First Series], (London, 1865).

23 James Mill, *op. cit.*, p. 17.

24 John Stuart Mill, *Principles of Political Economy, etc.* (London, 1891), p. 608.

25 Hume, "Of the Jealousy of Trade," *op. cit.*, III.

26 Hume, "Of the Balance of Trade," *op. cit.*, III, 365.

27 *The Wealth of Nations*, pp. 425-436, 507.

28 Ricardo, *op. cit.*, p. 83.

29 Hume, "Of the Rise and Progress of the Arts and Sciences," *op. cit.*, III, 133.

30 Hume, "Of the Liberty of the Press," *op. cit.*, III, 9; and "That Politics May Be Reduced to a Science," *op. cit.*, III, 15.

31 Quoted by Rae, *op. cit.*, p. 124.

32 James Mill, *op. cit.*, pp. 60-61.

33 Senior, *op. cit.*, I, 341.

34 Cannan, *op. cit.*, p. 251.

35 Hume, "Of Refinement in the Arts," *op. cit.*, III, 311-312.

36 Hume, "Of the Liberty of the Press," *op. cit.*, III, 12n.

37 Adam Smith, *Essays on Philosophical Subjects* (London, 1795), pp. 23, 25-27; *Lectures*, pp. 95, 160; *The Wealth of Nations*, p. 203.

38 Ricardo, *op. cit.*, p. 181.

39 M'Culloch, *op. cit.*, pp. 8-9.

40 *The Manchester School of Economics* (Stanford, 1960).

3   LIBERALISM IN THE GREAT CENTURY

1 John Ruskin, "Unto This Last," *Four Essays on the First Principles of Political Economy, Works* (New York, 1883), IX, 125.

2 J. E. Cairnes, *Essays in Political Economy. Theoretical and Applied* (London, 1873), pp. 248-249.

3 *Parliamentary Debates*, Vol. 101, pp. 638, 650.

4 *Report of Minutes in Evidence Taken by the Select Committee on the State of Children Employed in the Manufactories of the United Kingdom. Session 1816* (London, House of Commons, 1816), III, 10.

5   Herbert Spencer, *The Man versus the State* (London, 1884), pp. 5ff.

6   See, e.g., Oskar Lange, "The Political Economy of Socialism," *Science and Society*, XXIII (1959), 1-15; and Gyan Chand, "Poland's New Economic Model," *Indian Journal of Economics*, XXXIX (1958), 21-42.

7   Adam Smith, *The Wealth of Nations*, ed. Edwin Cannan (New York, 1937), p. 423.

8   J. R. M'Culloch, *The Principles of Political Economy, etc.* (2nd ed., London, 1830), p. 249.

9   William Smart, *Economic Annals of the Nineteenth Century* (London, 1910), I, 668.

10 Speech on the malt duty before the House of Commons, *Parliamentary Debates*, Vol. 182 (April 17, 1866), p. 1524.

11 Nassau W. Senior, *Letters on the Factory Act, etc.* (2nd ed., London, 1844), p. 10.

12 Quoted by Marian Bowley, *Nassau Senior and Classical Economics* (London, 1937), p. 265.

13 Cairnes, *op. cit.*, pp. 251, 244, 256, 260.

14 *Ibid.*, p. 251.

15 W. S. Jevons, *The State in Relation to Labour* (London, 1882), p. 33.

16 Spencer, *op. cit.*, pp. 105, 15-16.

17 On Spencer, see David Duncan, *The Life and Letters of Herbert Spencer* (London, 1908), pp. 319-320.
    On Locke, see John Adams, *A Defense of the Constitutions of Government of the United States, etc.* (London, 1794), I, 365.
    On Rousseau, see Kingsley Martin, *The Rise of French Liberal Thought*, ed. J. P. Mayer (New York, 1954), pp. 209-210.
    On Smith, see W. R. Scott, "New Light on Adam Smith," *Economic Journal*, XLVI (1936), 404.

18 John Stuart Mill, *Principles of Political Economy, etc.* (London, 1891), p. 604.

19 *Ibid.*, p. 609.

20 *Ibid.*, p. 614.

21 *Ibid.*, p. 627.

22 *Idem.*

23 Benjamin R. Twiss, *Lawyers and the Constitution. How Laissez Faire Came to the Supreme Court* (Princeton, 1942), pp. 141, 75-76n.

24 Mill, *op. cit.*, p. 604.